Charlie Brown's
Fourth Super Book of
Questions and Answers

about all kinds of people
and how they live!

Charlie Brown's Fourth Super Book of Questions and Answers

about all kinds of people and how they live!

Based on the Charles M. Schulz Characters

Random House New York

Editor: Hedda Nussbaum

Art Director: Eleanor Ehrhardt
Designer: Terry Flanagan
Layout: Charlotte Staub, Roberta Pressel
Picture Research: Anne Christensen
Production Director: Edward McGill

Special thanks to:

Dr. James Carse
Associate Professor of Religious Studies
The Kevorkian Center for Near Eastern Studies
New York University

David C. Gross
Associate Editor
The Jewish Week

Nathaniel Johnson
Senior Instructor
Department of Education
American Museum of Natural History, New York

Judith McGee
Assistant Curator
Costume Institute
Metropolitan Museum of Art, New York

Dr. Elliott Wright
Consultant in Religion
New York City

Photograph and illustration credits: American Airlines, 140 (bottom); © Marc and Evelyne Bernheim/Woodfin Camp & Associates, 124, 127, 128 (bottom), 129; the Bettmann Archive, Inc., 18 (bottom), 40, 41, 77; © British Crown, photo used by permission of Her Britannic Majesty's Stationery Office, 18 (top); British Tourist Authority, 39; David G. Brown, 43 (bottom), 115, 116, 117, 118, 119, 120; © Dan Budnik/Woodfin Camp & Associates, 52; Bureau of the Mint, 57 (top); Russell Burden, cover (top right), 53, 142; © C. Harrison Conroy Company, 68; Paul Cedfeldt, 16 (right); Anne Miller Christensen, 25 (top), 69; Colonial Williamsburg Photograph, 6; Philip Dion, 134, 136 (top), 138; Eleanor Ehrhardt, 5, 17 (bottom left), 88; Will Faller/Boy Scouts of America, 16 (bottom left); Terry Flanagan, cover (left), 7, 17 (middle right); French Government Tourist Office, 80; Marc Gave, 9 ("Lucy's Loom"); Greek National Tourist Organization, 39 (inset); Japanese National Tourist Organization, cover (top left), 24, 140 (top right); Kathleen Lane, cover (bottom right); George D. Lepp/ Bruce Coleman, Inc., 102; Light Opera of Manhattan, William Mount-Burke, producer/director, 19; Charles R. Luchsinger, 16 (top left), 17 (top right, middle left, bottom right), 63, 91; the Metropolitan Museum of Art, Bequest of Bashford Dean, 1929, 14; the Metropolitan Museum of Art, Mr. & Mrs. Isaac D. Fletcher Collection, Bequest of Isaac D. Fletcher, 1917, 67; the Metropolitan Museum of Art, Gift of Mrs. Loretta Hines Howard, 1964, 92; the Metropolitan Museum of Art, Gift of J. Pierpont Morgan, 1900, 83; the Metropolitan Museum of Art, Gift of William H. Riggs, 1913, and Fletcher Fund, 1921, 13; the Metropolitan Museum of Art, Rogers Fund, 1906, 3 (top); Mexican National Tourist Council, 140 (top left); Miller Services/Alpha Associates, Inc., 81 (inset); Museum of the American Indian, Heye Foundation, 10, 11, 12, 43 (top); National Gallery of Washington, Andrew W. Mellon Collection, *George Washington* (Vaughan Sinclair portrait) by Gilbert Stuart, 57 (bottom); the New York Historical Society, 35 (bottom); NFB Photothèque, photo by J. Feeney, 108 (bottom); NFB Photothèque, photo by Gabriel Gély, 109 (top); NFB Photothèque, photo by Kurt Kammersgaard, 81, 112; NFB Photothèque, photo by Scott Miller and David Hiscocks, 107; NFB Photothèque, photo by Terry Pearce, 111 (bottom left); NFB Photothèque, photo by D. Wilkinson, 108 (top), 109 (bottom), 111 (top right and left, bottom right); Meara C. Nigro, 86, 87; Peter Pernice, 51; Holly Pittman, 125; Belle Pressel, 91 (inset); Roberta Pressel, 90; Harold Roth, 73; Smithsonian Institution, Picture Collection of the Cooper-Hewitt Museum Library, 20, 35 (top), 46; Smithsonian Institution, National Portrait Gallery, 56 (bottom); Amidou Thiam, 3 (bottom); UNICEF, 22 (bottom); UNICEF/Water/Satyar, 22 (top); United Nations, 21 (top), 136 (bottom), 137 (top); United Nations/AID/Purcell, 21 (bottom); United Nations/FAO/H. Null, 133; United Nations/J. P. Laffont, 25 (bottom); United Nations/Kay Muldoon, 128 (top); United Nations/NAGATA, 126; United Nations/Philip Teuscher, 135; United Nations/Wolff, 137 (bottom); United Press International, 49, 56 (top), 78; United States Navy, 15, 17 (top left); © Wendy Watriss/Woodfin Camp & Associates, 54; © Martin Weaver/Woodfin Camp & Associates, 30, 31; Dennis W. Werner, 99, 100, 101, 103; The White House/Mary Anne Fackelman, 71; Wide World Photos, Inc., 55; © Adam Woolfitt/Woodfin Camp & Associates, 123.

Library of Congress Cataloging in Publication Data

Main entry under title: Charlie Brown's fourth super book of questions and answers. SUMMARY: Charlie Brown and the rest of the Peanuts gang help present a host of facts about how people live in various environments around the world. 1. Manners and customs—Miscellanea—Juvenile literature. 2. Human ecology—Miscellanea—Juvenile literature. 3. Ethnology—Miscellanea—Juvenile literature. [1. Manners and customs. 2. Human ecology. 3. Ethnology. 4. Questions and answers] I. Schulz, Charles M. II. Title. Fourth super book of questions and answers.
GT85.C45   390   78-68942
ISBN 0-394-84100-X   ISBN 0-394-94100-4 lib bdg.

Manufactured in the United States of America   3 4 5 6 7 8 9

Introduction

Welcome to *Charlie Brown's Fourth Super Book of Questions and Answers*. It's full of facts about people around the world yesterday and today—their holidays, their clothing, and how the places they live have affected their ways of life. When you look inside this book, you'll find answers to questions like these: How do desert people get water? Do all Eskimos live in igloos? Why do people wear green on St. Patrick's Day? How could knights move around in all that armor? Why do some people make a lot of noise on New Year's Eve? And many, many more.

And, as always, Charlie Brown, Snoopy, Lucy, Sally, Peppermint Patty, Linus, Woodstock, and the rest of the Peanuts gang are here to help out with the answers. So join them and start asking the questions!

Contents

Clothing Around the World
Yesterday and Today

Why do people wear clothes?

For many reasons. The most important one is protection. Winter clothes help protect people from the cold. Raincoats and boots keep them dry in rainy weather. Shoes protect their feet against hard rocks or hot sidewalks.

Most people are shy about showing their bodies to everyone around them.

People also wear clothes to tell others something about themselves. Some clothes show what a person does for a living. Police officers, nurses, and airline pilots, for example, wear uniforms to work.

The customs of different countries set fashions for clothes. In the United States brides wear white at weddings. In China brides wear red. Because of customs, people all over the world dress up in special clothes for holidays.

Dressing up helps people pretend. They may wear costumes and masks when they put on a play.

Last but not least, people wear clothes to help them look better.

What did the first clothes look like?

They were pieces of cloth or fur. People wrapped them around their waists, the way you wrap yourself in a towel. You've probably seen pictures of cave men dressed this way. To keep warm, people long ago wrapped other pieces of fur or cloth over their shoulders.

Another early form of clothing was the tunic (TOO-nik). People in Central Asia were wearing tunics 5,000 years ago.

What is a tunic?

A tunic is a long shirt that is made of two pieces of fur or cloth. One piece is for the front and one is for the back. The pieces are sewn together at the shoulders and at the sides.

Tunics can be long or short. In ancient Greece, more than 2,500 years ago, men wore tunics just above their knees. Women's tunics reached to the ground.

Ancient Greek vase showing warrior in tunic and short toga

Did the ancient Greeks wear underwear?

A poor person in ancient Greece had only one tunic—which was both underwear and outerwear. A richer person wore a tunic as underwear. Over the tunic, a rich Greek wore a himation (hih-MAT-ee-on), or toga.

What is a toga?

A toga is a large piece of cloth worn over one or both shoulders. Togas were popular for many hundreds of years in ancient Greece and Rome. During that time, toga styles changed a lot. But an ordinary man's toga was much smaller than a rich man's toga. A rich man wore his toga draped around his body many times. An ordinary man draped his only once.

Toga-like clothing is a style today in some parts of the world, especially Africa.

Woman from Senegal wearing togalike cloth over her shoulders

Most ancient Greeks went barefoot, even in the street!

When did men start wearing pants?

The first pants we know about for sure were worn 2,500 years ago in Persia (now Iran). Both men and women in ancient Persia wore pants.

The Persians traded with people from Central Asia. The Central Asians were nomads, people without settled homes. They lived in tents and moved from camp to camp. These nomads also wore pants. Today, no one is sure if the Persians copied the style from the nomads, or if the nomads copied the style from the Persians!

Who invented cloth?

No one knows. We do know that 5,000 years ago Africans were already making cloth from tree bark. Before Columbus discovered America, American Indians were also making bark cloth. It is possible that other people may have made cloth before either of these did.

To make bark cloth, both the Africans and the Indians laid wet pieces of bark across each other. Then they pounded the bark with rocks. The tiny fibers—hairlike pieces—that made up the bark stuck together. They formed a piece of cloth. West Africans still make bark cloth this way.

I GUESS I INHERITED THE TALENT FROM MY MOM.

Who invented thread?

Thread is made naturally by worms, insects, and spiders. The first human thread-makers probably got the idea for spinning thread from one of those creatures.

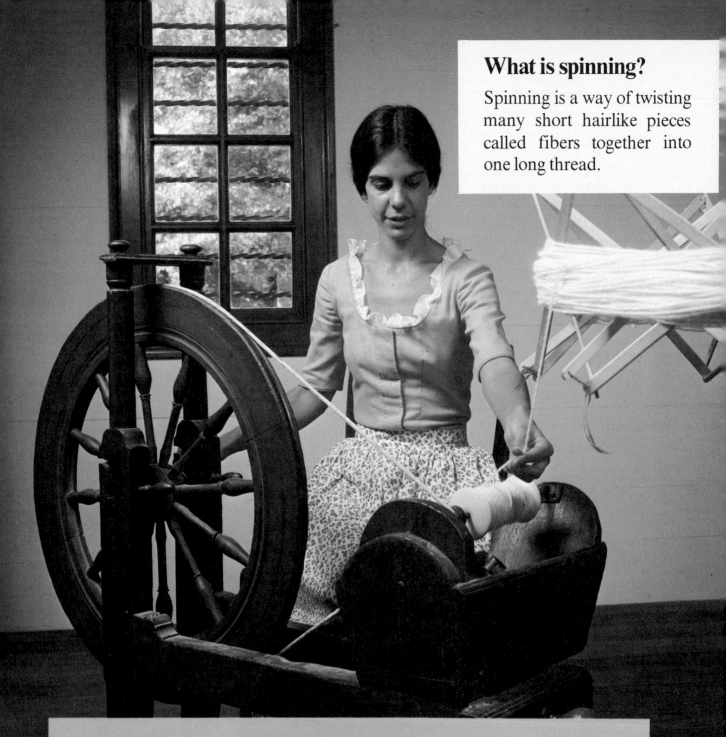

What is spinning?

Spinning is a way of twisting many short hairlike pieces called fibers together into one long thread.

How is spinning done?

For hundreds of years, people used a spinning wheel to make thread. It could spin only one thread at a time. Today modern factories use huge machines to spin hundreds of threads at a time. Here's how a thread is made.

The fibers are placed in a straight line. The end of each fiber overlaps the beginning of the next fiber. When the fibers are twisted, they cling together. The more the fibers overlap, the stronger the thread. Extra fibers can be twisted in to make the thread thicker.

What plant fibers are good for thread?

Any tall, stringy plant can be used to make thread. You can make thread yourself from tall grasses or cattails. Hang the plants in a cool, dry place for two or three weeks. They will become very dry. Then carefully pull apart the fibers and braid or twist them into thread.

Flax, hemp, and cotton are three plants grown for their fibers. From flax fibers we make linen. From hemp fibers we produce rope. From cotton fibers we make cotton cloth.

What animal fibers can be used for thread?

Thread can be made from the hair of any animal. People in ancient Asia used the hair of sheep, camels, and goats. Early South Americans used wool from wild mountain animals, such as llamas (LAH-muz), vicuñas (vye-KOO-nyuhz), and alpacas. These three goatlike animals still live in the Andes Mountains of South America.

North American Indians used horsehair, buffalo fur, and moose hair for thread making.

ISN'T THAT INTERESTING, SNOOPY? THEY CAN MAKE THREAD FROM DOG HAIR...

KLUNK!!

SUCH INSENSITIVITY BOGGLES THE MIND...

Could you make thread from your dog's hair?

You could if you had enough of it. But you'd need a lot of hair to spin enough for a piece of cloth. When your dog is shedding, you might sweep up the hairs and try it. But your dog would be VERY UNHAPPY if you tried it at any other time!

Indians in the American Northwest raised herds of dogs for their fur.

Who discovered how to make cloth from thread?

Probably fishermen in Egypt 5,000 years ago. They made fishnets by knotting and tying threads together. Nets were probably the first "cloth" made from thread.

Who invented weaving?

We don't really know. Weaving is a special way of putting together threads to make cloth. The process may have been discovered by net makers. Net makers tied the ends of their threads around weights. The weights kept the threads from getting tangled. The weights also made the threads hang tight and straight while the men were working. That probably gave someone the idea for a loom.

MY GRATITUDE TO THE WEAVER OF MY SECURITY BLANKET KNOWS NO BOUNDS...

8

What is a loom?

A loom is a machine for weaving. The loom keeps a whole row of threads tight and straight. The worker can then pass another thread in and out of the straightened threads.

People in Egypt were weaving more than 5,000 years ago!

Where did prehistoric people get needles for sewing?

Before metal was discovered, people carved needles from wood and bone. People that lived near the sea used fish bones and bits of shell. People in deserts used cactus spines.

Europeans were using metal needles about 2,500 years ago. Most American Indians did not have metal tools before the European settlers came to America just a few hundred years ago.

Where did American Indians get beads to decorate their clothes?

From the European settlers. Tiny beads for decoration were made in European glass factories. The Indians traded furs and blankets for the bright beads. They liked to sew the beads onto their clothes and weave them into their belts. Today beadwork is one of the best-known American Indian crafts.

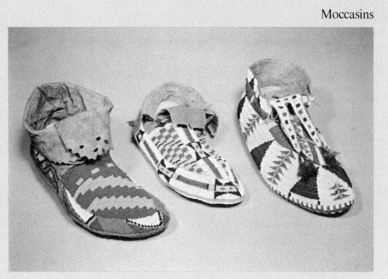

Detail of beading

Moccasins

What did American Indians wear before the settlers came?

Many Indian men and women wore leather tunics. They wore soft leather shoes called moccasins. In cold weather, they put on leggings—pieces of fur or leather which they wrapped around their legs. The leggings came up over their knees, like long socks.

How did American Indian styles change after the settlers came?

After meeting European women, Indian women in the northeast began wearing skirts and blouses. The fashion of cloth shirts spread among northeastern Indian men. In the southwest, Indian lands were settled by people from Spain. Spanish men wore long pants made of cloth. Soon the Indian men began to wear cloth pants, too.

Did the settlers get any styles from the Indians?

Yes. Daniel Boone and other pioneers dressed much like the Indians did. They wore long leather tunics, leggings, and moccasins. Their fur capes and leather bags copied Indian styles, too.

Leggings

Buckskin dress in tunic style

DON'T KNOCK IT TILL YOU TRY IT...

Indians and early settlers sometimes kept their feet warm in winter by stuffing the toes of their moccasins with grass!

What do Indians wear today?

Most American Indians wear the same kinds of clothes as other Americans. But for special ceremonies the Indians dress up in their traditional clothing.

11

Feather headdress

How did an Indian chief keep his war bonnet on during a battle?

He didn't have to—he didn't wear it! Its many feathers would just have been in the way! War bonnets were for special feasts and ceremonies. They were called war bonnets because the feathers and other decorations on them were prizes given for special deeds in war.

CAN I HELP IT IF THEY'RE MADE OF FEATHERS?...

What did the Indians wear in battle?

Some Indians fought in armor. Armor is a hard covering that protects a person in battle. The northwestern Indians made chest armor from thin strips of wood and leather. Around a warrior's neck was a wooden collar. It covered his chin and mouth, too. On his hair and forehead he wore a carved wooden helmet. It was in the form of either a fierce-looking person or an animal. The human face was supposed to scare the enemy. The animal face was supposed to bring the warrior good luck. The wood protected the man from clubs and arrows.

Other Indians fought bare-chested. They protected their chests with shields. A shield is a flat piece of armor that a warrior carries on his arm. Indian shields were often made of buffalo skins. The skins were dried to make them strong and hard.

Wooden helmet in shape of eagle

When did soldiers start wearing metal armor?

About 3,500 years ago. At that time soldiers in the Middle Eastern countries of Assyria (uh-SIHR-ee-uh) and Babylon (BAB-uh-lun) sewed small pieces of metal to their leather tunics. The metal gave warriors extra protection against enemy arrows. About 2,500 years ago the Greeks wore large pieces of metal on their chests and backs. They also wore metal helmets.

Much later, about 600 years ago, some soldiers in Europe called knights began to wear full suits of armor. A suit of armor covered a soldier's whole body with large pieces of metal joined together. The armor had hinges at the knees and the elbows. A heavy metal helmet covered the soldier's face, head, and neck.

WHY DO I LET HIM TALK ME INTO THESE THINGS?...

How could knights move around in all that armor?

Not very easily! Young knights had to train themselves to carry the extra weight. But their horses had the biggest burden. They carried the knights AND the armor. Often a knight's horse wore armor, too. Then the horse had to carry even more weight.

WHEN THEY TALK ABOUT THE GOOD OLD DAYS, I DON'T THINK THIS IS WHAT THEY HAVE IN MIND...

Armor for horse and man

13

What did ordinary soldiers wear?

Until 400 years ago, most common soldiers wore leather tunics and helmets. Sometimes the leather was covered with small pieces of metal. In some countries common soldiers wore chain mail under their tunics. Since their tunics had no sleeves, only chain mail covered their arms.

Some knights wore chain mail, too. But they wore it under a metal chest plate.

Did they get chain mail at the post office?

No. A soldier who wanted chain mail would visit the blacksmith's shop. Chain mail was a cloth made of small metal chains linked together. It protected the wearer from spears and arrows.

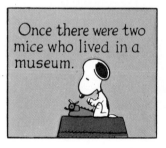

Once there were two mice who lived in a museum.

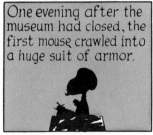

One evening after the museum had closed, the first mouse crawled into a huge suit of armor.

Before he knew it, he was lost. "Help!" he shouted to his friend.

"Help me make it through the knight!"

What do modern soldiers wear?

Soldiers now wear cloth uniforms. The color and style of the uniform show what country a soldier comes from. They also show in what branch of the armed services he or she is. The uniforms are sometimes decorated with buttons and bright patches.

SNOOPY, OL' PAL, MAYBE WE CAN BRING BACK THAT OLD STYLE AGAIN...

In the 1600s in Europe, people slashed up their clothes to be in style. They copied this fashion from soldiers whose clothes had been torn in battle!

United States Marines   *Insets*: Parachutist's Insignia; Navy Cross Medal

What do the patches on soldiers' uniforms mean?

Some patches tell a soldier's rank—how important that person is in the armed services. A beginning soldier might wear a patch with one stripe. A long-time soldier might wear a patch with eight or nine stripes. The uniforms of officers have metal bars and stars. A "four-star general" is one of the most important officers in the army.

Medals and patches also show what the soldier has done. Soldiers get medals for bravery and good service.

15

Do children wear uniforms?

Yes. Scouts wear uniforms. In most countries children wear uniforms to school. In the United States children who go to public schools don't wear uniforms. But many children in private schools do.

Are there other kinds of uniforms?

Yes. Here are some pictures of people wearing clothing that shows what kind of work they do.

Veterinarian

Navy crewman

Chef

Pilot

Minister

Maître d' (MAY-ter DEE)

Why do cooks wear tall white hats?

Cooks have been wearing white hats since at least 600 years ago. Back then most European workers wore special clothes as signs of their jobs. Bakers and cooks wore short, puffy white hats. Styles in cooks' hats changed over the years. In the 1900s cooks started wearing tall white hats with puffs at the end. The tall white hat is now the sign of any restaurant cook.

MEDIUM RARE, IF YOU PLEASE!

The Imperial State Crown of England

Why do kings and queens wear crowns?

A crown sets a ruler apart from ordinary people. A crown is a symbol that stands for power. Each crown has a design that represents its own country. When a country crowns its rulers, it gives them power over the country.

Kings and queens don't wear crowns all the time. Crowns are only for special ceremonies. Many crowns are heavy with gold and jewels. No person can wear one for more than a few minutes without getting a headache.

Some of the clothes of King Henry VIII (the Eighth) of England had so many jewels sewn on them that no cloth showed through!

King Henry VIII

Why do lawyers and judges in England wear white wigs?

The English lawyer's wig is a style left over from 300 years ago. At that time all important men in England wore wigs. The wigs had long curls that came down over the men's shoulders. Wig styles changed around the year 1700. The new style had hair pulled back in a ponytail. But lawyers and judges kept the older-style wigs as a sign of the importance of the law.

I CAN HEAR MY MOTHER NOW..."GET A HAIRCUT, SON..."

Performer wearing wig

 In the 1790s it was the style for men to put powder on their wigs.
Some wigs were powdered white.
Other wigs were light pink, silver, or blue!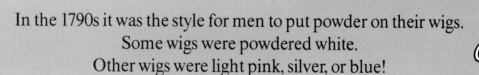

CLAP CLAP CLAP CLAP

THE COURT JESTER...

WHY CAN'T I HAVE A NORMAL DOG LIKE EVERYONE ELSE?...

PAWPET THEATER
The Foolish King
NOW PLAYING
EXCITING!
TERRIFYING!

Is it true that George Washington wore a wig?

No. People often say he did because wigs were in style for important men at the time of the American Revolution. Although many of the men who founded the United States wore wigs, Washington always wore only his own hair. He powdered it and pulled it back in a ponytail.

Hair styles worn by rich women in the 1770s were almost 3 feet high!

Do people still wear wigs?

Yes, many people do, often because they have lost their own hair. Modern wigs are supposed to look as much like real hair as possible.

20

Why do women in some countries wear veils?

Veils are supposed to keep men from looking at women. This custom is very old. Women were wearing veils in a Middle Eastern country called Ur 5,000 years ago.

A few religions forbid women to show their faces. Some women who belong to the Moslem faith cover every part of their bodies except their eyes.

Veiled women in Morocco

Veiled African man

Do any men wear veils?

Yes. Among the Tuareg (TWAH-reg) people of the Sahara desert, all men cover their faces. Women go without veils. Tuareg men believe they are more important than people who are not Tuareg. Ordinary people may not see their special faces.

Tuareg men wear their veils even when they eat and drink!

21

What else do people in the Sahara Desert wear?

Tuareg people wear sandals with big, wide soles shaped like paddles. The wide soles keep their feet from sinking into the sand.

They also wear what most desert people wear—loose clothes. Loose clothes allow air to reach a person's body easily. The air helps to keep the body cool in hot weather. Some desert people dress in long, flowing robes. Others wear loose shirts and trousers.

Desert dwellers protect their heads from the sun by covering them with cloth. Some desert men wrap their heads in turbans.

What is a turban?

A turban is a long piece of cloth that is wound around a person's head. Men wear turbans in Egypt, India, Arabia, and some other Asian and African countries. In some African countries, women wear turbans.

How do you get a turban to stay on your head?

Wrapping a turban is like tying a huge knot, with your head at the center. You pass the ends of the turban over and under each other. Then you tuck the ends of the turban under the folds of cloth.

There are hundreds of different ways to wrap a turban. The way one is wrapped sometimes shows what tribe or family a man comes from.

Turbans are sometimes fastened with a jeweled pin.

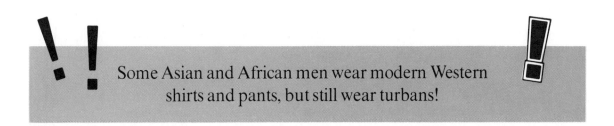

Some Asian and African men wear modern Western shirts and pants, but still wear turbans!

What do we mean by "Western" clothing?

By Western clothing we don't mean clothes that are worn back home on the range. We mean clothing styles that come from modern Europe or America.

Western clothes are shirts, dresses, pants, and skirts. Today these clothes are worn by people all over the world.

Even in Eastern countries such as Japan, most people wear Western clothes for everyday use. The native clothes, such as kimonos (kuh-MOE-nuhz) are now worn mostly on special occasions.

Kimonos

SCHROEDER.... IT'S TEA TIME!!!

What is a kimono?

The kimono is the traditional dress of the Japanese people. It is a long robe with wide sleeves and a wide sash. Both men and women wear kimonos.

Do Chinese people wear kimonos?

No. The kimono is a Japanese style. The Chinese used to wear robes, but they were different from kimonos—how different depended upon the part of China in which they were worn. Some Chinese robes had narrow sleeves and collars. Some had wide sleeves and no collars. Some had belts and others didn't. Some were worn over pants or skirts, and others were worn alone.

Performer wearing Chinese robe

Indian women wearing saris

What is a sari?

A sari is a long piece of cloth that women in India, Bangladesh, and nearby countries wear as a dress. It is usually made of silk or some other thin material.

Before dressing in a sari, a woman puts on a short blouse and a half-slip. Then she tucks one end of the sari into the top of the half-slip. She wraps the cloth around her body a few times and throws the other end over her shoulder. The bottom of the sari reaches to the floor.

What is a sarong?

A sarong is a long piece of cloth that is wrapped around the body once. Men and women who live on islands in the Pacific Ocean wear sarongs. So do some people of Southeast Asia. Men wrap their sarongs around their waists. Women wrap theirs under their arms.

Some people in Africa wear clothes that look very much like sarongs.

26

What is a muumuu?

Some women in Hawaii wear long, loose cotton dresses called muumuus (MOO-mooz). The style began when European and American settlers arrived in Hawaii in the 1800s. The newcomers thought that the Hawaiian women weren't wearing enough clothes. So they made the women cover up with muumuus.

IGNORE HIM, PATTY. PUT HIM NEAR A BEACH AND HE THINKS HE'S A HAWAIIAN PRINCE...

MUUMUU...RHYMES WITH WOO WOO— HI, SWEETIE!

27

What do Eastern people wear on their feet?

Most people in China, Japan, and other east Asian countries wear Western shoes. In other words, their shoes are much like yours. But sandals made of rope or straw are popular.

One style of Japanese sandal is the géta (GEH-tah). It has a very thick wooden sole called a "platform." Most gétas are only a few inches high. But when Emperor Hirohito (hear-o-HEE-toe) was crowned in 1926, he wore gétas almost a foot high!

In cold places such as Tibet and Mongolia, people wear boots of fur or heavy cloth.

People who live on the Pacific Islands often go barefoot. The weather is warm, and there are no hard, paved streets. So they have little need for shoes.

About 300 years ago, some European women wore shoes with platforms up to 30 inches (76 centimeters) high!

What do African people wear on their feet?

What they wear on their feet depends on where they live and how much money they have. Jungle dwellers need no shoes and go barefoot. Other Africans, too poor to buy shoes, also go barefoot. Some people can afford sandals. And in African cities, many people wear Western-style shoes. Much the same is true in South America.

Who invented raincoats?

Raincoats were probably invented by soldiers, shepherds, and other people who had to spend a lot of time outside in bad weather.

Cloaks were the first rainwear. A cloak was just a flat piece of leather or heavy cloth. Its owner may have rubbed animal fat into the leather to make it waterproof. When rain began to come down, he simply threw the cloak over his head.

What did cowboys wear when it rained?

In the days of the Old West, cowboys wore huge hats with wide brims. Cowboys and other ranch workers still wear them today. These hats are their main protection against rain, hail, snow, and sun.

29

Why do cowboys and cowgirls wear scarves around their necks?

The scarves that they wear are called bandannas. An old cowhand, J. Frank Dobie, once made a list of the uses of a bandanna. Here is the list:

1. Keeping the sun off the back of the neck.
2. Covering the nose on a dusty day.
3. Wrapping the ears in cold weather.
4. Tying on the hat in windy weather.
5. Blindfolding horses.
6. Wrapping a cut or wound.
7. Making a sling for a broken arm.
8. Straining mud out of stream water.
9. Covering the face of a dead cowboy.
10. Hanging horse thieves.

Today ranch hands probably use their bandannas for pretty much the same things—except, perhaps, hanging horse thieves!

Where did cowboy styles come from?

Cowboy styles came to North America from Spain. The Spaniards brought cattle with them. They also brought cattlemen. Spanish cattlemen wore wide leather hats called sombreros (some-BRAY-roes). They also wore leather vests, leather boots with metal spurs, and leather chaps.

Spur

What are chaps?

Chaps are heavy leg coverings that are worn on the outside of jeans or pants. They are made of tough leather. They protect the cowhand's legs from thorns and from cold when he or she is out riding a horse.

Cowboy in chaps

Do modern ranch workers wear chaps?

Yes, but North American ranch workers wear chaps less today than they used to. These people don't ride on horseback as much now as they did before. They often use cars instead. But in Argentina and Venezuela, two South American countries, there are many cowboys who do their work in the old-fashioned way. They still ride horses every day. So they need chaps.

Why do cowboys and cowgirls wear high-heeled boots?

High heels keep the feet of anyone on a horse from slipping out of the stirrups. If their feet aren't in the stirrups, riders can easily fall off their horses.

What other clothes did old-time cowhands wear?

When cowboys were working, they dressed in shirts and heavy work pants. Sometimes they put on an extra shirt to keep warm. Cowboys did not usually wear jackets on the job. They said jackets made their arms too hard to move. Instead they often wore vests.

Modern cowhands still wear the same kind of work clothes that old-time cowboys did.

When a cowboy of the 1850s or 1860s was finished with his work and had been paid, he often bought himself a new suit of clothes. Then he dressed in the latest style. No one could tell he was a cowboy.

What clothes were in style for men in the Old West?

Some men in the Old West copied the eastern styles. Men in eastern cities wore suits that had matching long pants and jackets. With the suits they put on fancy silk or velvet vests. They also wore white shirts, bow ties, and tall black hats called top hats.

Other men in the West dressed in fancy Indian-style clothes. Wild Bill Hickock, a famous frontier scout and marshal, was known for his fancy clothes. He wore Indian tunics of soft leather embroidered with beads. He carried silver guns with ivory handles.

What did women in the Old West wear?

A pioneer woman usually had only one good dress for going to church and to parties. The rest of the time she wore a blouse and a long cotton skirt. Sometimes in cold weather pioneer women wore leather leggings, like Indian women did.

Pioneer women also tried to keep up with the latest styles from back east. These included the newest fashions in bonnets and shawls. One popular style about 100 years ago was the very full skirt. Some of the skirts were so wide they couldn't fit through doors!

How did women get their skirts to be so full?

At first women made their skirts stand out by wearing many petticoats at once. But it was hard for women to get around that way. Their clothes weighed too much. So women started wearing hoop skirts to lessen the weight.

What is a hoop skirt?

A hoop skirt was a petticoat that looked like a cage. A woman wore her hoop skirt under a dress or skirt. The skirt covered the "cage." The hoop skirt held the skirt out much like a metal frame supports a lampshade. Some hoop skirts folded up when the woman sat down.

Since huge skirts got in the way, why did women wear them?

Because they wanted to be stylish. People have worn many very silly and uncomfortable styles over the years simply because they were in fashion.

What was probably the most uncomfortable style ever?

The hourglass waist. From the 1840s until the early 1900s people thought that beautiful women should have the shape of an hourglass. This means that they had to be very small in the middle and wide above and below that. Women wore either very full skirts or bustles. A bustle was a puff of cloth at the back of a skirt. It was often held up by a wire hoop. The hoop collapsed when the woman sat down. Women's waists were pulled in very tight with underwear belts called corsets.

A girl began tightening her waist when she was about 14. Every morning she put on her corset—even if she was playing tennis that day! As the girl grew older, her corset was laced tighter and tighter. It kept her waistline from growing. A few women's waists were only 12 or 14 inches around! Most modern women have waists at least 10 inches larger than that.

In the 1890s some five-year-old girls wore corsets!

LET'S HEAR IT FOR TODAY'S LIBERATED WOMAN...

Dress with a bustle

Wasn't it hard for women to breathe in tight corsets?

It certainly was. Corsets were both uncomfortable and unhealthy. That is why women began to talk about wearing more comfortable clothes. In 1850 Amelia Bloomer tried to get women to wear shorter dresses and roomy trousers—without corsets. People laughed at her idea. They called her trousers "bloomers." But Mrs. Bloomer won in the long run. About 50 years later, women got tired of not being able to move around. They started to wear simpler, looser clothes.

35

Is it true that women used to wear bathing suits with long pants?

Yes. In fact, in the 1850s and 1860s, women wore to the beach wool suits with long pants, full skirts, and high collars. And on their feet they wore canvas bathing slippers! If all that clothing got wet, it became very heavy. Anyone who tried to swim would sink!

Little by little, bathing suits got smaller and smaller. About 90 years later the bikini was invented. That barely covered up anything!

In most parts of the world, people always swam without ANY clothes on.

What did old-time bathing suits for men look like?

Most men didn't wear bathing suits at all until about the 1850s. At that time men and women started going to the beach together. At first the men wore just bathing trunks. But by the 1870s people were becoming more modest. So the men covered up with knitted tops that were like T-shirts. Their trunks reached to the tops of their knees. This style lasted for about 50 years.

When did women start wearing pants?

In many countries of the world, pants have been part of women's clothing for hundreds of years. But in Europe and the United States pants for women were not considered proper until the 1920s. Even the pants women wore as part of their bathing suits were mostly covered by their skirts.

Movie stars helped make pants popular in America. The stars wore loose pajamas of shiny materials for lounging at home or on the beach. By the 1930s women were wearing pants for sports and to parties as well.

While we were fighting World War II—from 1941 to 1945—many women worked in factories. They replaced men who had gone to war. The women factory workers wore overalls and other men's clothes. By the time the war ended, women were used to the comfort of pants. They began wearing pants more and more often. But until the 1960s most stores and offices did not allow women to wear pants to work. Now most women may wear pants whenever and wherever they like. Some schools still insist that girls wear skirts to class.

Do any Western men wear skirts?

Most Western men wear pants. But in a few countries men sometimes wear skirts. Their skirt styles are usually ones that have been worn in their countries for many hundreds of years.

For special occasions some Scottish men dress in knee-length skirts called kilts. Kilts are woven in brightly colored plaids. Each Scottish plaid belongs to a different family, or clan.

The guards at the Greek parliament building also wear kilts. The Greek kilts are white.

HERE'S JOE ZOOT GOING INTO TOWN ON SATURDAY NIGHT.

BUS STOP

Have men ever worn silly styles?

Yes. At various times, men have worn huge capes, very long feathers in hats, and tight starched collars. One of the silliest men's styles of recent times was the zoot suit. It was popular with some American men in the 1930s and 40s. The style called for a baggy jacket that reached to the knees and baggy pants that came up to the chest. The suit was usually dark-colored with thin light stripes. With it, men often wore a long chain that hung from the chest nearly to the floor. They usually put on suspenders to hold up the pants. And they topped off their outfit with a floppy hat.

  Men in the 1600s wore high-heeled shoes and silk stockings trimmed with bows and laces!

Are there people who don't wear any clothes at all?

Only a very few of the world's people go naked. These live in isolated parts of Australia, South America, and Africa. They belong to tribes that have not met many people from other places.

But even those who wear no clothes decorate their bodies. Some people in South America and Africa paint their bodies in bright designs. Others dress up for special occasions in colorful jewelry.

THERE ARE SOME PEOPLE IN THE WORLD WHO GO NAKED??... ...WELL THEY BETTER NOT SHOW UP IN THIS NEIGHBORHOOD OR 50¢ SAYS THEY'LL GET THROWN IN THE SLAMMER...

YES, MA'AM, I HAVE AN APPOINTMENT TO SEE THE DOCTOR...

WELL, IT ALL STARTED ONE NIGHT WHEN I COULDN'T SLEEP, AND I SAW THE SUN COME UP, ONLY IT WASN'T THE SUN...IT WAS A BASEBALL!

WHY DO I HAVE THIS SACK OVER MY HEAD? WELL, I'VE ALSO DEVELOPED THIS RASH OR SOMETHING, YOU SEE, AND...

MA'AM, DO WE HAVE TO DISCUSS THIS IN FRONT OF THE WHOLE OFFICE?

When did people begin wearing masks?

More than 10,000 years ago, cave people in Europe wore animal masks. Before a hunt, they held special dances. They believed the dances would help them have a good hunt. They wore masks to the dance. Some masks were of the animals the men were going to hunt. Other masks were of the gods in which the people believed.

The ancient Greeks wore masks on the stage 2,500 years ago. They put on plays in honor of their gods.

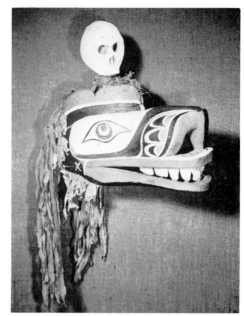

Indian wooden wolf mask

Have ordinary people ever worn masks on the street?

The ancient Greeks and Romans had masked holidays. On those days people would dress in costumes and masks. They would dance and play music in the streets. Masked holidays were great fun. With covered faces, people could go anywhere and do anything they liked. No one knew who they were.

The Greek and Roman holidays were much like the Mardi Gras (MAR-dee-grah) today. A Mardi Gras is held every winter in New Orleans. Another takes place in Rio de Janeiro, Brazil. People wear funny costumes and masks in the streets.

Of course, as all trick-or-treaters know, children wear masks in the streets every year on Halloween.

Performers wearing masks in festival in Nepal

Do people ever wear masks in everyday life?

Masks are worn for many sports. Skiers sometimes wear knitted wool masks. The masks are like socks, with holes for the skiers' eyes, nose, and mouth.

Divers wear masks underwater. Baseball catchers wear masks made of metal and leather. Bank robbers wear masks, too.

Why do catchers wear masks?

Catchers wear masks to protect their faces. When the batter hits a foul ball, the ball can come right at the catcher's face. A fast baseball can badly hurt someone who gets hit in the face with it.

GET THE PUCK!

PASS! SHOOT! CHECK 'IM!

KNOCK HIM DOWN! SHOOT! CLEAR IT! MOVE! SKATE WITH IT!

HIT HIM! SHOOT!!

SKATE! SKATE! ALLONS! ALLONS!

Why do some athletes wear shoulder pads?

Football is a very rough game. The padding protects the players if they get hit or knocked down. Hockey players also wear padding to protect them from falls.

Do people wear padding in ordinary clothes?

Yes. Jackets and coats are often padded in the shoulders. In the 1940s stylish women's jackets had big pads in the shoulders. The pads made their shoulders look wider.

When did Western men start wearing jackets?

The modern jacket came into use in England on December 15, 1660. Before then Englishmen wore short capes. They copied the style from the French and bought many capes made in France.

King Charles II (the Second) of England wanted his people to stop buying clothes from France. So on December 15, 1660, he appeared in court dressed in a Turkish-style jacket. He knew that everyone would copy his style and give up French capes.

The King of France was angry at Charles's fashion change. To get even, he made all the servants in the French court wear jackets.

When did long pants come into fashion for men?

Around 1800. Before that time, long pants were worn only by common work-ingmen. Rich men wore knee-length pants over stockings.

In 1789 a revolution began in France. The common people overthrew their rich rulers. After that no one wanted to look rich. All men began wearing long pants, which were ordinary working clothes.

 The zipper did not become popular until 1931! Before that, people fastened their clothes with buttons and hooks.

OH, YOU HANDSOME DOG, YOU!

Why do styles change?

In the past, people copied the clothes of the kings, queens, and people of the court. And some styles changed by royal order, as in the case of jackets in France.

Sometimes styles have changed after two different groups of people met. One copied the other. In colonial America, settlers and Indians traded styles. Today people all over the world copy styles from the United States. Blue jeans, T-shirts, and tennis shoes are a few of the imitated fashions.

Styles are also set by the people who design, make, and sell clothes. Ordinary people would not buy new clothes as often as they do if styles did not change.

What will clothes look like in the future?

We don't know exactly what styles people will wear. Fashion changes in strange ways. But in the future we may wear fewer clothes. We probably won't need heavy winter coats. Scientists in the space program have invented new types of cloth. One type is a warm, lightweight cloth used for astronauts' clothes. Even now, raincoats and other clothes are made with various kinds of cloth invented by the space program.

Some clothes in the future will probably be "unisex" clothes. That means both men and women can wear them. Jeans and T-shirts are some of the "unisex" clothes that people wear today.

Has New Year's Day always been January 1?

No. Most countries in Europe did not make January 1 the first day of the new year until about 1600. England waited until 1752. Before those dates, the Christian countries of Europe celebrated the new year on March 1 or March 25, at the start of spring. In some parts of the world today, people celebrate the new year when the first green of spring appears.

January 1 was the first day of the new year in the Roman calendar. That calendar was very much like the one we use today. About 40 years before Jesus was born, it was put into use by Julius Caesar (SEEZ-ur). But people thought New Year's should be in March. So the idea didn't really catch on for many hundreds of years.

Times Square, New York City, on New Year's Eve

Why do some people make a lot of noise on New Year's Eve?

Thousands of years ago people believed that evil spirits roamed the earth. They thought that the spirits were especially dangerous at the new year. People made loud noises at the moment the new year began to scare away the evil spirits.

Most of us don't believe in evil spirits anymore. But we still make loud noises when the clock strikes twelve on New Year's Eve. Blowing horns and shaking rattlers and noisemakers are a lot of fun.

Why do people make New Year's resolutions?

People want the new year to be filled with happiness. So they resolve, or decide, to make some improvements in themselves starting January 1.

Resolutions go back a long way in New Year's celebrations. The month of January is named for the ancient Roman god Janus. He was the god of doorways and beginnings, and of comings and goings. Whenever Romans started anything new they made sacrifices to Janus. This means that they took flowers, fruits, or animals to a temple that honored Janus. The Romans always sacrificed to Janus at the start of the new year. They hoped the sacrifice would bring them the god's favor in the months ahead.

Resolutions can be a kind of sacrifice, a promise to give up something even if it is only a bad habit.

How do the Chinese celebrate their new year?

The Chinese New Year's Eve and New Year's Day are quiet family days. Then the celebrations get livelier. There are parades almost every day. Musicians, clowns, and dancers in the parades do funny things that make people laugh. The celebration lasts 15 days.

Americans celebrate Chinese New Year

How does the Chinese New Year celebration end?

With the Festival of Lanterns. The Chinese make beautiful lanterns from silk, papier-mâché (PAY-pur muh-SHAY), and glass. They shape some to look like cars, fish, dragons, animals, airplanes, and Chinese houses. The lanterns hang outside houses and in gardens. They hang along streets and in front of shops and temples. Some stay up during the whole 15-day celebration. People add still more for the festival.

When the sky gets dark on the festival day, the people parade with many lanterns. Boys wear fantastic costumes and prance about on stilts. The highlight of the evening is a papier-mâché dragon. It is often as long as a passenger-train car. Sometimes it takes as many as 50 men and boys to carry the dragon along.

 In Burma, people celebrate the new year by throwing water on each other!

SPLASH!

51

What is Rosh Hashanah?

Rosh Hashanah (ROASH-huh-SHAH-nuh) is the start of the Jewish New Year. It means "Head of the Year" in Hebrew. Rosh Hashanah is always either in September or October. Some Jews observe it for one day, but for most it is a two-day holiday. Rosh Hashanah is the beginning of the Ten Days of Repentance (rih-PENT-unts). During these days, Jewish people think about their lives. They repent, or feel sorry about their sins. They look for ways to improve themselves.

On Rosh Hashanah, Jews pray in the synagogue (SIN-uh-gog), the Jewish house of worship. After the synagogue service, they gather with their families for a festive holiday dinner.

Inside of synagogue

How do Jews observe Yom Kippur?

Yom Kippur (yom KIP-ur), or the Day of Atonement, is the most sacred day of the Jewish year. It is the day on which Jews atone, or make amends with God, for their sins of the year just past. It marks the end of the Ten Days of Repentance. Jews who are 13 years old and over fast on Yom Kippur. They do not eat or drink anything for a whole day. The day begins just before the sun goes down on Yom Kippur. It ends just after sundown the next day.

On the eve of Yom Kippur, the synagogue service begins with the chanting of a prayer of repentance, Kol Nidre (COLE NID-ruh). Many Jews spend the rest of the evening and most of the next day praying in the synagogue. Yom Kippur ends at sundown with the blowing of the shofar (SHOW-far).

What is a shofar?

A shofar is a musical instrument made from a ram's horn. It sounds something like a trumpet or a few oboes played together. The shofar that Jews used thousands of years ago could be heard for miles. Sometimes it warned people of danger. It also told people when to go to the temple to pray. The modern shofar is smaller and not as loud. Jewish people listen to the sound of the shofar on Rosh Hashanah and Yom Kippur. It reminds them to think seriously about their lives.

Cantor blowing a shofar

 On Rosh Hashanah people eat pieces of apple dipped in honey—sweet food to start off a sweet year!

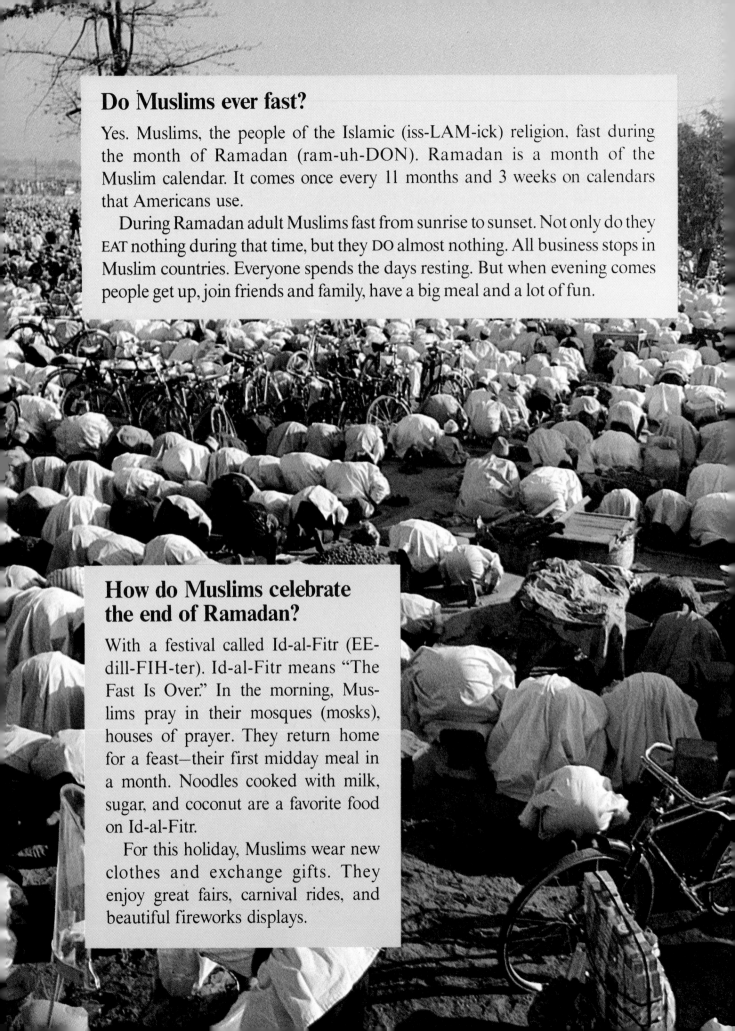

Do Muslims ever fast?

Yes. Muslims, the people of the Islamic (iss-LAM-ick) religion, fast during the month of Ramadan (ram-uh-DON). Ramadan is a month of the Muslim calendar. It comes once every 11 months and 3 weeks on calendars that Americans use.

During Ramadan adult Muslims fast from sunrise to sunset. Not only do they EAT nothing during that time, but they DO almost nothing. All business stops in Muslim countries. Everyone spends the days resting. But when evening comes people get up, join friends and family, have a big meal and a lot of fun.

How do Muslims celebrate the end of Ramadan?

With a festival called Id-al-Fitr (EE-dill-FIH-ter). Id-al-Fitr means "The Fast Is Over." In the morning, Muslims pray in their mosques (mosks), houses of prayer. They return home for a feast—their first midday meal in a month. Noodles cooked with milk, sugar, and coconut are a favorite food on Id-al-Fitr.

For this holiday, Muslims wear new clothes and exchange gifts. They enjoy great fairs, carnival rides, and beautiful fireworks displays.

What happens on Ground Hog Day?

According to an old tradition the ground hog, or woodchuck, wakes up from its winter sleep on February 2. The animal is supposed to come out of its hole and become a weather forecaster. If the ground hog sees its shadow, the story goes, it becomes frightened and goes back into the den for more sleep. This is supposed to mean six more weeks of winter. But if the ground hog doesn't see its shadow, it won't be frightened. It stays up to search for food. This is supposed to mean spring will be coming soon.

Who brought the Ground Hog Day tradition to America?

Both the Germans and the English. For hundreds of years Germans have watched the badger on February 2. They say the badger's behavior on that day will tell them whether spring is coming early or late. The English have watched the hedgehog for the same reason. German and English settlers in America began watching the ground hog to continue the tradition.

55

Opposite: Nigerian Moslems bowed in prayer

What is Martin Luther King, Jr., Day?

It is a special day to remember Martin Luther King, Jr., a famous black American civil rights leader and minister. He worked peacefully to bring about equal rights for black Americans. Many states honor the memory of Martin Luther King, Jr., on January 15, his birthday.

Do all Americans celebrate Lincoln's Birthday?

No. Only 25 states of the United States celebrate Lincoln's Birthday, February 12, as a separate holiday. Four more states put Lincoln's Birthday and Washington's Birthday together into President's Day. Some Southern states don't celebrate Lincoln's Birthday at all because Lincoln was President during the Civil War. At the start of that war, the South withdrew from the United States. President Lincoln's army fought the Southern army and brought the South back into the country.

56

When is Susan B. Anthony Day?

On her birthday, February 15. Susan B. Anthony was an American who lived in the 1800s. At that time women were not allowed to vote in elections. Susan B. Anthony fought very hard to get women that right. In 1872, she voted and was arrested for it. When she died in 1906, only four states had given women the right to vote. Today every woman in every state has that right.

POWER TO MY KIND!

When do Americans celebrate George Washington's Birthday?

George Washington was born on February 22. But his birthday is now celebrated on the third Monday in February. In this way people can enjoy a long weekend with the holiday.

George Washington was the first President of the United States. He was also Commander in Chief of the army during the American Revolutionary War. Americans fought that war so that they could rule their own country. George Washington is the only American president so far whose birthday people celebrated while he was still alive.

Who was St. Valentine?

Nobody knows for sure, and there are several saints named Valentine. One St. Valentine was a priest and doctor. He lived in the city of Rome about 300 years after the birth of Jesus. The emperor of Rome refused to allow people to be married in a Christian ceremony. St. Valentine ignored the emperor. He continued to perform marriages in the Christian way. When the Romans found out, they sent St. Valentine to prison and executed him. Later, February 14 became St. Valentine's Day, a day to honor one of the St. Valentines. Still later it became simply Valentine's Day, a day for sweethearts.

When did people begin sending valentines to each other?

People started writing valentine love letters in about 1400. Soon some began to draw pictures on their letters. They added lace to make their valentines prettier. Once people sent valentines only to their sweethearts. But today people send valentines to friends and family, too.

Valentine's Day is very popular in England, France, the United States, and Canada.

Why do Irish people celebrate St. Patrick's Day?

St. Patrick is the patron saint of Ireland. He introduced Christianity to Ireland. St. Patrick's Day is both a holy day and a national holiday in Ireland. It is popular also in American cities in which many Irish families live. A lot of non-Irish people enjoy it, too. St. Patrick's Day is March 17, the anniversary of his death more than 1,500 years ago.

Was St. Patrick Irish?

No! St. Patrick wasn't born in Ireland. He was probably born in Wales. He called himself "Patricus," a Latin name which means "well-born." Patricus is Patrick in English.

St. Patrick went to Ireland as a slave. He had been captured by Irish raiders who knew nothing of Christianity. Later he escaped and returned to his home where he became a Christian bishop. He went back to Ireland to teach Christianity to the people there.

Why do people wear green on St. Patrick's Day?

St. Patrick's Day is an Irish holiday, and green has almost always been connected with Ireland. Perhaps this is because the hills of Ireland look so green. There is a legend that says that in Ireland's landscape there are 40 shades of green. Also, shamrocks, small three-leaved plants, grow wild in Ireland and stay green the year round.

Did St. Patrick drive the snakes out of Ireland?

There are no snakes in Ireland today. A legend says that St. Patrick drove them out by beating on a drum. However, some people believe that Ireland never had any snakes.

Snakes have long been connected with evil and evil doings. St. Patrick was a good man. So some people think the legend means that St. Patrick drove evil out of Ireland.

What is Lent?

Lent is the time each year when Christians prepare themselves for Easter. It is the 40 days (not counting Sundays) from Ash Wednesday to Easter Day. The 40 days remind Christians of the time Jesus spent praying and fasting in the wilderness.

The word "Lent" comes from an old word for spring, "lengthentide," when the days are lengthening (growing longer). Lent begins in February or early March depending on when Easter Sunday itself comes.

A long time ago Christians followed strict rules of fasting during Lent. They did not eat anything with eggs, milk, meat, or animal fat in them. The rules are less strict today. But Christians are still expected to live simply and to ask God's forgiveness for their sins.

Lent is a time when Christians are expected to think about the needs of other people. As a sign of their faith, some people deny themselves (give up) a favorite food or activity for 40 days. Sharing whatever is given up is another chance to help people in need.

Why do some people have ashes on their foreheads on Ash Wednesday?

Christian churches have special Ash Wednesday services at the start of Lent. In some churches, ashes are used to mark small crosses on the foreheads of the people. Ashes are an ancient symbol of sorrow. They remind people to be sorry for their sins during Lent.

The ashes used in churches on Ash Wednesday are made by burning the palm branches used on Palm Sunday the year before. Palm Sunday is the Sunday before Easter.

What do pretzels have to do with Lent?

At one time Christians ate pretzels only during Lent. Pretzels are made from plain dough sprinkled with salt. They have no milk, eggs, or animal fat—foods Christians were not supposed to eat as they prepared for Easter.

"Pretzel" comes from a Latin word for "little arms." The twist in the thin bread looks like arms folded in prayer.

Some people in Europe still never eat pretzels except during Lent.

What do hot cross buns have to do with Lent?

Hot cross buns are sweet cakes decorated with a sugar cross on top. Many Christians eat them during Lent.

Hot cross buns were first baked in Europe. Nobody knows exactly when. One tradition dates the custom from 1361 when a Christian monk baked hot cross buns to give to poor people.

What is Mardi Gras?

Mardi Gras (MAR-dee grah) is a festival day on the Tuesday before the beginning of Lent. The Mardi Gras celebration began in France. It is the day that ends a season of parades, parties, and carnivals.

"Mardi Gras" means "fat Tuesday" in French. It dates from the time when Christians had to use up all animal fat before Lent. From early January until the night before Ash Wednesday, the French people would celebrate. The biggest festival of all was on "fat Tuesday."

Today, Mardi Gras carnivals are popular in many European cities. Rio de Janeiro, Brazil, has a grand carnival, too.

Some Christians call the day before Lent begins Shrove Tuesday. "Shrove" is an old word that means "to confess sins." On Shrove Tuesday people would go to church, confess their sins, and then go home for a big party.

Do any people in the United States celebrate Mardi Gras?

Yes. French settlers brought the Mardi Gras festival to the United States. Cities in Alabama, Florida, Louisiana, Mississippi, and Texas have colorful Mardi Gras celebrations. The biggest is in New Orleans, Louisiana. Many families of French background still live there.

How do people in New Orleans celebrate Mardi Gras?

With a carnival that lasts for ten days. People come from all over the United States to join the fun. They wear masks and fancy costumes, go to parties and balls, and watch parades. Groups called Krewes sponsor the events. Each Krewe names a king and queen for its parade, a custom dating back hundreds of years to carnivals in Europe.

The biggest parade and parties are on the last day of the carnival. A Krewe called the Rex Organization ("Rex" is a Latin word meaning "king") chooses the king of the whole carnival. There is a parade with bands and gigantic floats. Huge torches light the floats. Everyone wears a mask—except the king of the carnival—and dances until dawn.

What is Pancake Day?

People in England celebrate Pancake Day on Shrove Tuesday, the day before Lent begins. Long ago Christians were not supposed to eat fats, milk, and eggs during Lent. So they make pancakes to use up those foods.

Children in England like to play toss-the-pancake on Pancake Day. Someone throws a pancake high in the air. Children jump up and try to grab it. Whoever catches the biggest piece of pancake wins a prize.

What is a Pancake Day Race?

A Pancake Day Race takes place in Olney, England, every year. Women run carrying a frying pan in which a pancake is still cooking. They must flip the pancake three times during the race. Each racer wears a hat, and an apron over her dress. Slacks are not allowed. The winner receives a kiss from the person who rings the bell to start the race. Winner and runner-up each receive a prayer book.

Some people say the custom began in 1445. On the day before Lent began, people were on their way to church. A woman making pancakes heard the church bell ring. She ran to church still wearing an apron and holding the frying pan in her hand.

Do people in the United States celebrate Pancake Day?

Yes. The townspeople of Liberal, Kansas, hold a Pancake Day Race. The winner gets prizes. After the race is over the people of Liberal, Kansas, talk by telephone to the people of Olney, England.

What is Holy Week for Christians?

Holy Week is the week before Easter. It begins on Palm Sunday, another joyful day for Christians. On Palm Sunday, many churchgoers receive branches or leaves of palm trees. The palms remind Christians of Christ's triumphal entry into the city of Jerusalem. There, a few days before his death, he was hailed as a king. The joyous crowd who greeted him strewed his path with palms.

Monday, Tuesday, and Wednesday of Holy Week have no special names. Thursday is called Maundy (or Holy) Thursday. "Maundy" comes from a Latin word used in a hymn often sung on the Thursday of Holy Week. Maundy Thursday keeps the memory of the Last Supper when Jesus introduced Holy Communion. Jesus and his disciples (dih-SIE-pulls)—his closest followers—were all Jews and celebrated Passover. The Last Supper was a Passover meal that Jesus ate with his disciples.

Good Friday is the saddest day of the year for Christians. On Good Friday, Christians remember the crucifixion and burial of Jesus. Such a sad day is called "good" because of all the good that Jesus brought into the world. The Greeks call the day "Great Friday."

The day before Easter is Holy (or Low) Saturday. Churches have no services that day. Some drape their doors in black cloth. The black represents the time Jesus spent in his tomb.

Portrait of Christ by Rembrandt

Why do Christians celebrate Easter?

Easter is the happiest and most important Christian holy day. On Easter Christians celebrate their belief in the resurrection (rez-uh-RECK-shun) of Jesus Christ on the third day after his crucifixion (crew-suh-FIK-shun). "Resurrection" means "a rising from the dead." "Crucifixion" means "being put to death on a cross."

The Christian religion teaches that Jesus's resurrection is a great victory over death. It brings new and everlasting life to all who believe in Jesus.

The English word "Easter" probably comes from "Eostre," the name of an old goddess whose festival was in the spring. Easter is always in the spring.

Easter celebration at St. Patrick's Cathedral, New York City

68

Why does the date of Easter change from year to year?

Because Easter was first celebrated according to the ancient Jewish calendar—not the Roman calendar used today. Easter is always on Sunday. But it can come as early as March 22 or as late as April 25.

For a long time, Christians observed Easter at the same time that Jews celebrated Passover. Passover can begin on Sunday, Tuesday, Thursday, or Saturday. The Christians wanted Easter on Sunday since they believe Jesus rose from the dead on the first day of the week. The Christians were also slowly giving up the use of the Jewish calendar in favor of the Roman one. So in the year 325, the Christians made a change. They decided on a formula for setting the date of Easter. Easter is the first Sunday following the first full moon in the spring.

Why is the egg an Easter symbol?

In many of the world's cultures the egg stands for new life. An egg looks like a stone or a rock. But it is from an egg that new life bursts forth. The egg is a reminder to Christians of the resurrection of Jesus.

When did people begin to decorate eggs at Easter?

No one is certain. Some people think the Egyptians colored eggs in the spring long before Jesus was born. Before dye was invented, people colored eggs by wrapping them in leaves and flowers and dropping them in boiling water. This gave the eggs the color of green leaves or red petals. Later, Christians painted eggs and had them blessed. They ate some and gave the others to friends as Easter gifts.

How do people in Europe decorate Easter eggs?

Germans decorate empty eggshells. First they make a tiny hole in each end of a raw egg. Next they blow the egg out of its shell. Then they color the outside of the unbroken eggshell. Greek Christians exchange bright-red eggs. The people who live in the Ukraine (you-CRANE), a part of the Soviet Union, decorate Easter eggs with pictures. Some are of fir trees, bell towers, or chapels.

Why does the Easter bunny carry colored eggs?

In many cultures, the white hare—like the egg—stands for new life. There are many old stories about hares and eggs.

A German legend says that a poor woman once hid colored eggs in a nest. They were to be an Easter gift for her children. Just as the children saw the nest, a hare hopped away. So people said the hare brought the eggs.

Today people call the Easter hare the Easter bunny.

What happens on the day after Easter in Washington, D.C.?

Children roll Easter eggs on the White House lawn. Dolly Madison began the custom when her husband, James, was president (1808–1816).

Children try to roll their hard-boiled eggs as far as possible without breaking them. There are no other rules for egg rolling. As many as 50,000 people watch or take part in the event. Many hope to get a look at the president, who comes out to watch.

Easter-egg-rolling contest at the White House

What is an Easter parade?

It's a parade of people, all dressed up for Easter. Many people wear new clothes on Easter. After church some of them go for a walk. Europeans used to say prayers and sing religous songs on Easter walks. Today people call an Easter walk an Easter parade. There is no music at an Easter parade. People just walk up and down the street. In years when hats are in style, women show off their fancy Easter bonnets. Sometimes famous people join the Easter parade on Fifth Avenue in New York City.

71

What is Passover?

Passover is a happy Jewish holiday. It celebrates the Jews' escape from slavery in Egypt more than 3,000 years ago. For most Jews the holiday lasts eight days. During that time they eat special foods, such as matzos (MOTT-suhz), that remind them of their ancestors' escape. Jewish families invite their relatives and friends to join them on the eve of the first two days for a seder (SAY-dur), a special meal and religious service.

What happens at a seder?

During a seder, Jewish people sit around the dining table and read aloud from a book called the Haggadah (huh-GAH-duh). It tells the story of the Jews' slavery and escape to freedom. "Haggadah" means "story" in Hebrew. On the table are a plate of matzos and a plate of special foods: horseradish; parsley or celery; a mixture of wine with crushed apples, almonds, and cinnamon; a lamb's shankbone; and a roasted egg. They are symbols of Jewish slavery and deliverance. The seder also includes prayers, songs, and a big Passover meal.

What do the special foods on a Passover table stand for?

Each of the special foods on the seder plate stands for something else. The horseradish, called maror (mah-RORE) in Hebrew, is a bitter herb. It reminds Jews of the bitterness of slavery in Egypt. It also recalls the bitter fate of those modern Jews who live in countries that don't allow them to follow the laws of their faith.

The parsley or celery, called carpas (CAR-pahss), is a reminder of the poor food supply the ancient Jewish slaves lived on. During the seder ceremony, a piece of carpas is dipped into salt water. The salt water stands for the tears of the slaves.

The wine-apple-almond-cinnamon mixture is called haroset (har-O-set). It represents the mortar, or cement, that the Jewish slaves had to mix as they worked for their Egyptian masters.

The shankbone stands for the lamb that was offered by Jews as a sacrifice to God in ancient days. The roasted egg, still in its shell, is a symbol of a special sacrifice offered during early Passover celebrations. The egg is called baitza (bait-ZAH).

Why do Jewish people eat matzos on Passover?

Eating matzos reminds Jews of their escape from slavery in Egypt. During that escape, the Jews had no time to bake bread. Bread needs time to rise, or puff up, before it is baked. So the Jews baked flat breads, without yeast. They were something like matzos, which are also made without yeast.

Dinner table set for Passover seder

What is Arbor Day?

Arbor Day is a special day for planting trees. There is no set date for Arbor Day in the United States. But many states celebrate Arbor Day in May. The first Arbor Day celebration in the United States took place in Nebraska on April 10, 1872. On that day people in Nebraska planted a million trees. Some holidays celebrate the past, but Arbor Day is dedicated to the future. Trees prevent floods and keep the topsoil from blowing away. A tree is the symbol of life in many cultures.

How did April Fools' Day get started?

No one is sure how April Fools' Day got started. Most countries seem to have a day when people play tricks on each other. Children especially like these days.

Some people think that trick days began in India. People there celebrate a spring holiday called Holi (HOE-lee). A favorite trick on Holi is to fill a bamboo pipe with colored powder and blow the powder at people. Sometimes children fill the pipe with water and squirt each other.

How do people in Japan celebrate Buddha's Birthday?

People in Japan celebrate Buddha's (BOO-duz) Birthday with a flower festival on April 8.

Buddha was a great religious leader in India. He lived about 500 years before Jesus was born. He taught people to stay calm and to be kind to one another. In that way, he said, they could find peace and happiness. His followers spread his teachings throughout Asia.

On Buddha's Birthday millions of Japanese Buddhists go to their neighborhood temples carrying fresh flowers. There they wash a small statue of Buddha with sweet tea. Little girls cover their faces with white powder so they will look clean and fresh for Buddha. Children wear silk kimonos (robes) that are decorated with fresh flowers. Buddhist priests march through the streets wearing costumes of olden days. Many floats pass by in a parade. One float always carries a statue of Buddha on a huge white elephant. In India only important royalty were allowed to ride on white elephants. The statue of Buddha on an elephant shows how important he is to the Buddhists.

What is May Day?

It is an ancient holiday in which people dance around a large pole with streamers hanging down. The pole is called a Maypole. May Day is celebrated on May 1 in many countries of Europe.

When did Americans start celebrating Mother's Day?

The first Mother's Day celebration in the United States took place in 1873 in Boston. But it was not until 1915 that Mother's Day became a national holiday. Ever since then Americans honor their mothers on the second Sunday in May.

When did Americans begin to celebrate Father's Day?

People in Spokane, Washington, celebrated the first Father's Day in 1910. Mrs. John Brice Dodd, who lived in Spokane, thought that fathers should be honored with a special day. She talked to her minister about it. He, a few other ministers, and the YMCA convinced people to celebrate Father's Day. The idea spread to other cities and states. In 1924 President Coolidge asked people all over the United States to honor their fathers with a special day. Ever since then, Americans celebrate Father's Day on the third Sunday in June.

Why do Canadians celebrate Victoria Day?

Canada is part of the British Commonwealth—a group of countries that either are or once were under English rule. Victoria Day celebrates the birthday of Queen Victoria. She ruled England and the Commonwealth for 64 years (1837–1901). After she died, people continued to celebrate her birthday, May 24. Modern Canadians celebrate the holiday on the Monday that comes just before May 25. In this way, Canadians have a long holiday weekend.

Is there a Children's Day?

Yes. Many Protestant churches in the United States celebrate Children's Day. It is the second Sunday in June. Children who belong to the church take part in religious programs—songs, stories, and plays. On that day, the children are sometimes promoted from one Sunday school class to the next.

Throughout history other countries have celebrated special children's days in various ways. One unusual custom is practiced in Yugoslavia. Parents tie up their children on that country's Children's Day. They set the children free when they promise to be good for the rest of the year.

How do Americans honor the men and women who served in wars?

The United States has two holidays to honor people who were part of the armed services. Veterans Day, November 11, honors all men and women who served in the army, navy, marine corps, and coast guard. Memorial Day honors American soldiers who died in wars. Memorial Day used to be called Decoration Day because people decorated the graves of soldiers with flowers. It is celebrated on the last Monday in May.

Most Southern states have their own Memorial Day. Many celebrate it in April or May. On this holiday Southerners remember soldiers who fought in the Civil War—a war in which the Southern states fought the Northern states. On Memorial Day, they decorate the graves of soldiers who fought for the South.

Canadians have a holiday a lot like Memorial Day. It is called Remembrance Day. This holiday is celebrated on the same day as Veterans Day in the United States. It is the day World War I ended.

Marine Corps War Memorial, Arlington, Virginia

How do French Canadians celebrate Jean Baptiste Day?

People who live in Quebec celebrate Jean Baptiste (ZHON-bah-TEEST) Day on June 24 with a parade. Quebec is the French-speaking area of Canada. A favorite float in the parade shows a little boy dressed as a shepherd. He is Jean Baptiste, St. John the Baptist, the patron saint of Quebec. A lamb with a ribbon and bow around its neck stands next to St. John. The lamb stands for Jesus. Great crowds gather in the city of Montreal and cheer little St. John and his lamb.

The Jean Baptiste holiday begins on June 24 and lasts eight days. During that time French-Canadians in Quebec honor the French language and culture.

Why do people in the United States celebrate the Fourth of July?

The Fourth of July is the birthday of the United States of America. In the 1700s, England ruled over 13 colonies along the east coast of what's now the United States. The colonists thought that the English king treated them unfairly. They wanted to rule themselves. In 1776 a group of leaders from the colonies met in Philadelphia. They talked about independence from England. Thomas Jefferson wrote down their thoughts in the paper called the Declaration of Independence. It said that the colonists wanted to be free, and it told why. The Fourth of July was the day the Declaration of Independence was finished. Four days later it was read to a large crowd of people. Bells rang and the people cheered. A new country was born. But it had to fight and win a war with England before it became a free country—the United States of America.

Bastille Day parade, Paris

Why do the French celebrate Bastille Day?

The Bastille (ba-STEEL) was a French prison. The French king sent many people there who displeased him. On July 14, 1789, French rebels attacked the prison and freed the prisoners. They destroyed the Bastille. The capture of the Bastille by the rebels stands for freedom to the French people. Bastille Day is a great national holiday in France. The French celebrate it with music, parades, and dancing in the streets.

When do Americans celebrate Flag Day?

People in the United States celebrate Flag Day on June 14. On that day in 1777, leaders of the American colonies voted to accept a new flag as the symbol of their country. Before that they flew the Grand Union flag. It had a small design of the English flag on it. The new flag had 13 stars on it instead—to stand for the 13 colonies.

There is a legend of how a seamstress named Betsy Ross made the first American flag. The story goes that General George Washington wanted the stars to have six points. But Betsy talked him into using five-pointed stars instead.

When do Canadians celebrate Dominion Day?

Canadians celebrate Dominion Day on July 1. Dominion Day is Canada's birthday. Like the United States, Canada was once ruled by England. On July 1, 1867, the English decided to make Canada into a dominion. A dominion makes its own laws. But it is still loyal to another country (like England) that has a king or queen. Some Canadians call Dominion Day "Canada Day." On that day Canadians display flags and watch parades. The Canadian mounted police wear their bright red jackets.

Celebration in Ottawa, Canada

What is Labor Day?

The United States and Canada have their own day to honor workers. It is called Labor Day. The word "labor" means "work." Labor Day is celebrated in both countries on the first Monday in September.

Is there a holiday for pets?

Yes. In the United States, there is a National Pet Health Week in October. During that week people are reminded to have their pets checked by an animal doctor every year. In September there is a Pet Responsibility Week. The purpose of that week is to remind people to learn how to take good care of their pets.

Why do people in North and South America celebrate Columbus Day?

To honor Christopher Columbus, who landed in America on October 12, 1492. Many people say that Columbus was not the first European to discover America. The Irish and Norwegians claim their explorers came to America first. But no one paid much attention to their discoveries. Columbus's discovery caused Europeans to realize that a new land—America—existed.

 Columbus didn't know that he discovered America. He thought he'd landed near China or Japan!

Why do people celebrate Halloween?

Halloween is a combination of holidays. As a night of ghosts and witches it was started by the Celts (selts). They were people who lived in France and the British Isles hundreds of years ago.

The Celts had a holiday called Samhain (SAH-win), which meant "end of summer." So Samhain was a festival marking the end of the food-growing season. The Celts believed that spirits of the fruits and vegetables, and also the ghosts of people, visited the earth on Samhain, which was October 31. The Celts lit huge bonfires on hilltops to scare the ghosts away.

Years later, the Celts became Christians. They and other Christians celebrated Allhallows Day (now called All Saints' Day) on November 1. It was a day to remember important Christians who had died. The Celts called the night before (October 31) Allhallows E'en, or holy evening. "Allhallows E'en" was later shortened to "Halloween."

Many of the customs of Samhain were continued on Halloween. Almost all spooky Halloween practices were started by the Celts.

Why did people believe that witches traveled on broomsticks on Halloween?

In Europe a few hundred years ago, there were people who called themselves witches. They worshiped the devil the way most people worship a god. They claimed they could perform witchcraft, or magic. The witches held large meetings called Sabbats. There they gathered around a big fire where they cooked up magical potions. Some of these were drugs the witches drank. Sometimes the drugs caused them to imagine themselves flying through the air. There were always brooms near the fire to sweep it clean. So stories got started that witches used magic to fly about on broomsticks.

The Sabbat held on Allhallows E'en was a special one. People believed that the witches flew to this Sabbat on broomsticks.

I'M KIDDING! I'M KIDDING!! THERE'S NO SUCH THING AS WITCHES. OR GHOSTS OR GOBLINS.

How did trick or treat get started?

Trick or treat began in Ireland. People went from house to house and begged for food on Halloween. They promised good luck to those who gave and bad luck to those who didn't.

Who was Jack-o'-Lantern?

To the Celts, Jack-o'-Lantern was the spirit of the pumpkin. The Celts carved a pleasant-looking pumpkin face to show Jack as a good spirit, not a nasty one.

The Irish claim that Jack-o-Lantern was a person who couldn't get into heaven because he was too stingy. But the devil didn't want him, either. So ever since, he's had to wander about carrying a lantern. The Irish had no pumpkins, so they used to make Jack-o'-Lanterns from turnips and potatoes.

Why do people wear spooky costumes on Halloween?

The custom of wearing spooky costumes on Halloween began with a group of Irish Celts called Druids. The Irish believed that evil spirits roamed about the earth on Halloween. The Druids wanted to fool the evil spirits into thinking that they were spirits, too. So they dressed as ghosts and goblins.

Is there really a Great Pumpkin?

Not even Linus can answer that question. And he's been waiting for the Great Pumpkin to show up for years!

Jack-o'-lantern

Why do people in England celebrate Guy Fawkes Day?

Guy Fawkes Day, November 5, celebrates the capture of an English traitor named Guy Fawkes. In 1605, he and some friends planned to blow up the Houses of Parliament with the king inside. (Parliament is something like the Congress of the United States.) Someone wrote a letter to a member of Parliament. It warned him of the plot. Searchers discovered 36 barrels of gunpowder in the cellar. They arrested Guy Fawkes just as he was about to light the gunpowder. He and his helpers were executed.

The Clock Tower of the Houses of Parliament

How do the English celebrate Guy Fawkes Day?

With mischief making! At night people march in noisy parades. Children ring bells, crash cymbals, and bang pots. They make a great deal of noise. People stuff a dummy of Guy Fawkes with straw and burn it on top of a large bonfire. They light firecrackers. They sing and yell while Guy Fawkes burns.

When is Election Day?

The Tuesday after the first Monday in November is Election Day in the United States. Election Day is a legal holiday in most states. That means people get the day off from work and school. Every four years United States citizens vote for a new president and vice-president. During other years, they vote for state governors, city mayors, or judges. Sometimes they vote for members of Congress.

In Canada and England there is no regular national election day. National elections in Canada and England can be called at any time.

Why do we eat turkey on Thanksgiving Day?

Eating turkey on Thanksgiving is a tradition that started when the Pilgrims ate turkey on the first Thanksgiving. The Pilgrims were a group of English people who came to America in 1620. During their first winter in their new land, they didn't have enough food. Many died. But that spring, their Indian neighbors taught them to plant corn. The Indians showed the Pilgrims where to catch fish. They taught the Pilgrims how to use fish to make the soil richer. By fall, it was clear there would be plenty of food for the next winter.

Because they were thankful, the Pilgrims decided to have a feast—the first Thanksgiving celebration. This took place in 1621. And what better way to celebrate than with plenty of food! The Indians were invited to the feast, of course.

For the occasion, the Pilgrim men hunted deer and turkeys. Turkeys ran wild during those days. Somehow, the tradition lasted, and we eat turkey every year on Thanksgiving Day.

 Benjamin Franklin loved turkeys. He wanted the turkey to be the national bird of the United States.

Do Canadians celebrate Thanksgiving?

Yes, on the second Monday in October. Canadians claim that the first Thanksgiving ever celebrated in North America took place in Canada in 1578. In both Canada and the United States, people celebrate Thanksgiving in much the same way. Turkey is a favorite food in both countries.

Menorah

Why do Jewish people celebrate Hanukkah?

Hanukkah, or Chanukkah, (HAH-nuh-kuh), celebrates a victory and the rededication of the Jewish temple more than 2,500 years ago. In the second century before Jesus was born, a Greek ruler in Syria had taken over the Jewish land where Israel is now. He had also taken over the Jews' temple in Jerusalem. For three years the Jews fought until they won back their temple and some of their land. They rededicated the temple to God.

The Jews wanted to relight their temple lamps, which the invaders had let go out. But there was only enough holy oil for one day. A legend says a miracle happened. The lamps were lit and that tiny bit of oil burned for eight days. By then, more holy oil had been made. Because of this, Hanukkah is also called the Festival of Lights.

Hanukkah comes during the month of December. People celebrate it for eight days in memory of the eight days that the oil burned.

How do Jewish people celebrate Hanukkah?

Every night of Hanukkah, Jews light candles and recite special festival blessings. The Hanukkah candle holder is called a menorah (muh-NOR-uh). A menorah has space for nine candles—one for each night of Hanukkah plus a shammash (shah-MASH), or a serving candle. On the first night, one candle and the shammash are lighted. Each night one more candle is lighted. On the last night, all the candles are burning.

During Hanukkah, Jews eat special holiday foods, usually cooked in oil. Many eat potato pancakes called latkes (LAHT-kuz). They sing songs and exchange gifts. Children receive Hanukkah gelt—money. Sometimes they also get pieces of chocolate wrapped in gold foil that look like gold coins. And they have fun playing with a top called a dreidel (DRAY-dill).

Dreidel

When did people begin to celebrate Christmas?

No one knows the day and month of Jesus's birth. It was a long time before Christians had a set date for celebrating Christmas. About the year 350, a church in Rome decided Christ's Mass, a church service marking the birth of Jesus, should be on December 25. This became popular. People called Christ's Mass "Christmas."

The Christmas tree at The Metropolitan Museum of Art

Who decorated the first Christmas tree?

No one knows for sure. The custom of bringing an evergreen tree indoors and decorating it at Christmas started in Germany. One legend says that Martin Luther started the practice. Luther was an important Christian leader. According to the story, he noticed the starlit sky as he walked home one Christmas Eve about the year 1513. He thought the stars looked as if they were shining on the branches. When he arrived home, Martin Luther placed a small fir tree inside his house. He decorated it with lighted candles.

Decorating Christmas trees became popular in Germany. Prince Albert, the German husband of Queen Victoria, took the tradition to England. Both German and English people brought it to America.

Did people always sing Christmas carols?

Christmas has had its own music and songs since it started. But Christmas carols have a special history. The word "carol" means "circle dance." Among many ancient people, caroling was common at festivals. Groups would dance arm-in-arm, often singing simple, happy songs. Carols became a natural way for Christians to express their joy at Christmas.

Christmas carols were known in England by the year 1100. St. Francis of Assisi (uh-SEE-zee), who lived in Italy about 800 years ago, encouraged the singing of Christmas carols. He is sometimes called the Father of the Christmas Carol.

What special game do Mexican children play at Christmas?

They like to break the piñata (peen-YAH-tuh). A piñata is a clay pot that Mexicans make in many shapes. Sometimes a piñata looks like a fat person, a clown, an animal, or Santa Claus. It is filled with Christmas treats such as candy, nuts, and small gifts.

Someone hangs the piñata from the ceiling or a doorway. It is just above the children's reach. A leader blindfolds them one at a time and leads them to the piñata. Everyone hopes to get a turn. The leader gives the blindfolded child a stick. The child takes three swings at the piñata while the other children circle around it. They dance and sing.

When the piñata breaks, everyone scrambles for the Christmas treats.

Who was the first Santa Claus?

Many people say that Nicholas, the bishop of Myra, was the first Santa Claus. Nicholas lived in what is now part of Turkey about 300 years after Jesus was born. Very little is known about him. But he is supposed to have loved children and to have given them presents.

Nicholas became a popular saint in Europe. He is the patron saint of Russia. His special day is December 6. "Santa Claus" is the English for "Sinter Claes," the Dutch name for St. Nicholas.

Did people always believe that reindeer pulled Santa's sleigh?

No. Through the years people have believed many different things about how Santa Claus traveled. Some people believed that Santa traveled on a donkey or a horse. Others believed that he traveled across the sky in a chariot pulled by horses. But people who lived in Scandinavian countries were always certain that Santa traveled in a sleigh pulled by reindeer. How else could he travel through icy Northern Europe?

What is a Yule log?

A Yule log is a big log of wood that some people burn on Christmas Eve. Before the time of Jesus, Scandinavians had a holiday called Yule. They celebrated Yule at about the time of year that people today celebrate Christmas. On Yule they lighted huge logs. The fires were supposed to make the sun shine brighter. After Scandinavians became Christians, they continued to burn Yule logs. The custom of burning Yule logs at Christmas spread throughout Europe, including England.

WAIT 'TILL YOU SEE OUR YULE LOG...IT MUST WEIGH TWENTY POUNDS.

TWENTY POUNDS!! SOME DOGS JUST CARRY IN THE NEWSPAPER...

What's the best holiday of the year?

Everybody has his or her own favorite holiday. Snoopy likes Easter because he gets to play the role of the Easter Beagle. Lucy likes April Fools' Day. She enjoys fooling Charlie Brown. Charlie Brown doesn't like any holidays. They remind him of the cards he never gets!

How People Live in the Rain Forest

The Amazon Indians of Brazil

What is a rain forest?

A rain forest is a very warm, very rainy place where many trees grow. Because of the rain, the trees grow tall and close together. The covering of treetops is so thick that it blocks the wind. The air is still and uncomfortable. The thick treetops also keep sunlight from reaching the ground. Most plants need sunlight to live. So in much of the rain forest, few low plants can grow. It is quite easy to walk through these areas.

A rain forest has more than a lot of trees. It also has many different kinds of animals. These include noisy birds, hungry crocodiles, anteaters, lizards, snakes, and big cats called jaguars.

Unfortunately, the list also includes thousands of different kinds of insects. Army ants eat anything that doesn't move out of their way. Certain mosquitoes give people diseases that can kill them. Sweat bees crawl into people's ears and noses. Ticks and flies bite their skin.

Is a rain forest the same as a jungle?

No. A jungle is part of a rain forest—the thickest part. It usually grows up in places where people have cut down the tall trees. Then many ground plants grow quickly. In fact plants grow on, around, and over one another. They tangle into each other. Because of this, a jungle is a very hard place to walk through.

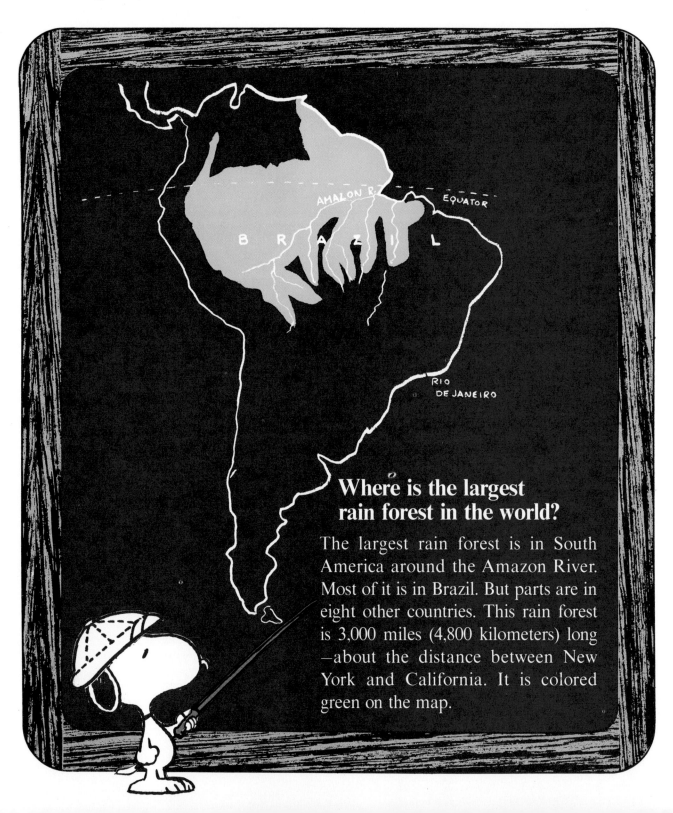

EQUATOR

AMAZON R.

B R A Z I L

RIO DE JANEIRO

Where is the largest rain forest in the world?

The largest rain forest is in South America around the Amazon River. Most of it is in Brazil. But parts are in eight other countries. This rain forest is 3,000 miles (4,800 kilometers) long —about the distance between New York and California. It is colored green on the map.

Who lives in the Amazon rain forest?

Tribes of people we call Indians. These people are distantly related to the Indians of North America. But they look very different. They have darker skins and shorter bodies than North American Indians. Because they live in a rain forest, their way of life is very different from those Indians who live in Arizona, California, or Maine. Their languages are different, too.

Until recently, the Amazon Indians lived exactly as their ancestors had thousands of years ago. The rain forest kept them separated from the rest of the world. Today, Indian life is slowly changing.

Flooded rain-forest path

How much rain falls in the Amazon rain forest?

A lot! In the wettest places about 100 inches (250 centimeters) of rain falls in a year. That is more than twice the rainfall of New York City each year. And it's more than six times as much as a year's rainfall in Los Angeles.

In the rain forest the wettest months are called the rainy season. Then heavy rain falls during part of every day. The rest of the year is the "dry" season. But even that is not very dry. It's just less wet.

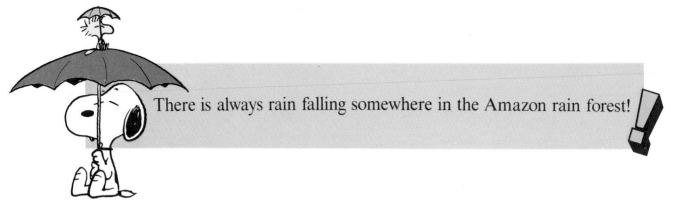

There is always rain falling somewhere in the Amazon rain forest!

What kind of houses do Amazon Indians build?

Some Indians build houses that look like haystacks. These are made of dried palm leaves or dried grasses. A frame of thin poles holds the "hay" in place.

Other Indians use the dried palm leaves for roofs only. They make the walls of their houses from either thin tree trunks or mud.

What's the inside of a rain forest house like?

Each house has one very big room. The floor is a natural dirt floor. The room has some stools made from tree trunks. It has hammocks to sleep in. There are no windows, so the house is dark. Sometimes the Indians build a fire inside to cook their food. But most of the time they do their cooking outdoors.

Who lives in each house?

In many Amazon houses parents, children, grandparents, aunts, and uncles all live together. Sometimes as many as 70 people live in one house! Each set of parents and young children has a part of the big room to themselves.

What do rain forest people eat?

They eat many kinds of fruits and vegetables. They grow some in their gardens and gather some in the forest. They add to their diet by hunting and fishing.

Corn and cassava (kuh-SAH-vuh) are the most important crops in the Amazon rain forest. (Cassava is the plant from which tapioca pudding is made.) The Indians make cakes from dried and grated cassava roots. They roast corn, and they make a soup of ground corn. The Indians also raise and eat sweet potatoes.

Trees of the forest supply the Indians with fruit and nuts. Bees provide them with honey. Some tribes are always on the lookout for a tree with a bee's nest in it. When they see one, they chop it down. They build a smoky fire near the tree to drive the bees away. Then they take the honey from the nest. They eat it, and they drink it mixed in water.

Amazon Indians also eat wild pigs, monkeys, armadillos (are-muh-DILL-oze), turtles, and many kinds of fish. They usually roast the meat and fish over an open fire, barbecue style.

Amazon Indians carrying racks of live turtles to another village

MONKEYS... THOSE PEOPLE EAT MONKEYS?!!

Amazon waters have piranha (pih-RAHN-yuh) fish in them. One piranha can fit in your hand. But a group of piranhas could eat you up in just a few minutes!

Do the Amazon Indians hunt with guns?

Yes. Sometimes they use shotguns to hunt large ground animals. But for hunting birds, fish, and other small animals the Indians stick to their old ways. They use spears, blowguns, or bows and arrows.

A blowgun is a long, hollow bamboo pole. Through it an Indian blows poison darts.

The Indians are very skilled hunters. They can hit fast-moving animals with their arrows and darts. They can even hit fish with their arrows!

Rain forest hunters use bamboo stems to make long arrows. Sometimes the arrow tips are made from the wood of a palm tree. Some bows are as long as 6 feet (2 meters). They may be longer than the hunter! The hunter makes his bow strings from thin strips of palm wood.

HERE'S THE WORLD-FAMOUS HUNTER ON A MOTH CHASE!

Some Amazon Indians hunt at night with the help of modern flashlights!

Is it true that rain forest Indians are unfriendly?

Some of them are. In the past, hunters and explorers hurt and killed many of them. In the early 1900s some were forced to work as slaves by people who came to take rubber from the forest's rubber trees. Because of these things, some Indians dislike strangers.

Other Amazon Indians are shy rather than unfriendly. They are frightened by visitors, who are very different from themselves. Often, though, these Indians learn to trust visitors and accept them as friends.

Man standing by pool with bow and arrow

Tribal chief wearing special ornaments

Is it true that Amazon Indians wear no clothes?

Many rain forest Indians wear little or no clothing. Some wear only belts, armbands, jewelry, or headbands. Some wear only tiny skirts called loincloths.

For special occasions these Indians paint their bodies with dyes made from jungle plants. They use many different colors and designs. Some of the designs stand for animals of the rain forest.

Child wearing beads and feathers

Man dressed for a festival

Amazon mask and costume

103

Who teaches the rain forest children?

Mostly parents, friends, relatives, and older children. But they don't teach reading, writing, and arithmetic. Instead, children learn skills they will need when they grow up. Girls learn how to search for honey and fruit, plant crops, and cook. They also practice weaving cloth and caring for younger children. Boys learn to hunt and fish.

There are a few modern schools in the Amazon rain forest today. They were set up by the government of Brazil. In these schools, children read books and take tests—just as you do.

Do Amazon children have time for toys?

Yes, they do. But they have to make their own. Sometimes their parents help them. They use cornstalks, bits of wood, bones—whatever they can find. They turn these things into dolls, toy animals, and balls.

In an Indian relay race each man who runs carries a 100-pound (45-kilogram) log on his shoulders!

What happens when people get sick in the rain forest?

Many Amazon Indians believe that evil spirits cause illness. When these Indians are sick, they call in a shaman (SHAY-mun). Shamans are very important people in a rain forest village. They are supposed to be able to see and control evil spirits. Shamans try to drive evil spirits out of a sick person's body to make the person well.

For a long time scientists didn't believe a shaman could really cure a sick person. But most have changed their minds. Doctors and dentists now use as medicines many of the plants shamans have used for a long time.

Jungle villages do not have modern doctors and nurses. However, doctors and nurses sometimes visit the rain forest to take care of sick Indians. The doctors are Brazilians. But they are not Indians. However, there are now some Indian nurses and medical teams.

How People Live in Very Cold Lands

Eskimos of the Arctic

What are the coldest places in the world?

The Arctic (ARK-tick) and the Antarctic (ant-ARK-tick). The Arctic is the area around the North Pole. It is usually colder than the inside of your home freezer! During an arctic winter the temperature sometimes goes as low as −60°F. (−51°C.).

The Antarctic is the snow-and-ice-covered land around the South Pole. It's even colder than the Arctic—so cold that temperatures there have to be measured on special thermometers.

The Arctic and the Antarctic are called the polar regions.

Does anyone live in the world's coldest places?

Some birds, seals, fish, whales, insects, and spiders live in parts of the Antarctic. But no people do. Scientists from a few countries sometimes visit there to learn more about the area. But they usually stay less than a year. People do live in the Arctic. They are called Eskimos (ES-kuh-moze). About 50,000 Eskimos live in northern Canada, Alaska, and on the island of Greenland. Maybe 1,500 more live in the arctic areas that belong to Russia.

 There are about 120 times as many people in New York City as there are Eskimos in the whole world!

Is there a summer in the Arctic?

Yes. But summer never gets very hot—not even in the southern parts of the Arctic, where it is the warmest. The average summer temperature there is only as warm as spring in Chicago, Illinois. That's about 50°F. (10°C.). And the temperature often drops below freezing. Snow sometimes falls during the summer. In the southern part of the Arctic, the summer snow melts fairly soon. But the ground is always frozen below the surface. This frozen area is called the permafrost.

Only strong plants can grow during the short, cool arctic summer. In spite of this, there are several hundred different kinds of arctic plants.

 Eskimos make a natural freezer by simply digging a hole in the ground.

> DON'T TELL ME...LET ME GUESS.... IT SNOWED LAST NIGHT!

> WOODSTOCK! I WONDER WHAT HAPPENED TO WOODSTOCK!

> POOR WOODSTOCK DOESN'T KNOW HOW TO TAKE CARE OF HIMSELF IN EMERGENCIES...

> HE'S PROBABLY SNOWED UNDER, OR FROZEN STIFF, OR...

How do Eskimos keep warm?

By bundling up. In winter they wear warm fur clothing and sleep under fur blankets.

In very cold weather Eskimos put on two of everything. They wear the fur of the first layer of clothing against their skin. They wear the fur of the second layer on the outside.

An Eskimo wears fur boots called mukluks (MUCK-lucks). Their outer soles are made from the skin of a moose or seal. Their tops are made from canvas or caribou (KAR-uh-boo) skin. A caribou is a kind of deer that lives in the Arctic.

In an igloo, an Eskimo family sleeps on a bed made of snow blocks!

Do all Eskimos live in igloos?

No. In fact, very few modern Eskimos live in them. But most know how to build igloos from snow blocks. Only in Canada do some Eskimos still live in igloos for most of the year. During the short summer, they move into tents made from animal skins.

Most Eskimos today build houses of stone or wood. There is plenty of rock in the Arctic. So building stone is easy to get. But wood is hard to find and expensive to buy. Trees cannot grow in the Arctic because of the cold and the permafrost. Eskimos who live near water often collect and use driftwood that washes up on the shore. It is carried by the ocean from places south of the Arctic. Other Eskimos buy logs or boards for their houses. They are brought by ship from faraway places. That's why they are so expensive.

Modern houses with electricity and oil furnaces are recent. They mark a great change in the lives of the Eskimo people.

109

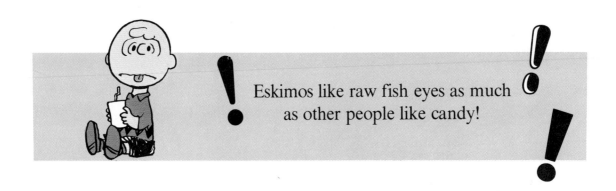

Why don't igloos melt when Eskimos cook their food?

Because cooking doesn't produce enough heat. An Eskimo family that lives in an igloo uses a small saucer-shaped lamp as a stove. It burns animal fat and gives off enough heat to cook meat and fish. It even gives off enough heat to make the igloo a little warmer. But the temperature inside the igloo stays below freezing. So the snow blocks can't melt. The Eskimos must wear their fur clothing inside the igloo.

Some Eskimos use their lamps for warmth and light only. They eat their food raw.

How do Eskimos travel in the snowy Arctic?

Like many things in Eskimo life, travel is a mixture of the old and the new.

At one time Eskimos did all of their traveling in sleds pulled by dogs. Some Eskimos still travel this way. But many use snowmobiles with gasoline engines instead.

For travel on water, Eskimos use motorboats, kayaks (KIE-aks), and umiaks (OO-mee-aks). Both kayaks and umiaks are made of animal skins stretched over a wooden frame. Eskimos move them by paddling.

For long trips Eskimos often travel by airplane. Small planes fly regularly between many places in the Arctic. Some planes use skis instead of wheels for landing and taking off.

Eskimo sled

Eskimos and sled dogs watching approach of an airplane

Kayaks

Snowmobiles pulling sleds across ice

Do Eskimos have doctors and dentists?

Yes, they have both. In the past, few doctors and dentists were Eskimo. But that is changing. More and more young Eskimos are studying medicine and dentistry. They go to school in the United States, Canada, or Denmark.

In most Eskimo villages, there is no permanent doctor's or dentist's office. About once a month a doctor travels by airplane to visit a village. The doctor sets up an office in a government building. People from that village and nearby smaller ones come to the office. After a day or two, the doctor leaves. Dentists visit in the same way.

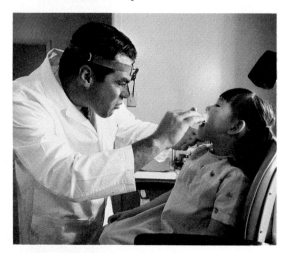

When Eskimos are very sick, an airplane takes them to a hospital. Modern Eskimos have better health care than they ever did. Yet, they are not as healthy as they used to be. Visitors to the Arctic have brought germs that make Eskimos sick. Some of the modern food that Eskimos buy harms their teeth. So arctic doctors and dentists have plenty of patients.

Do all Eskimos hunt and fish?

No, not anymore. Until just a short time ago, all Eskimo men were hunters and fishers. The only ways Eskimos could get meat and fish were by hunting and fishing. And these were also the only ways Eskimos could get skins for clothing, blankets, and boats.

Today, they can buy most things at stores or through mail-order catalogues. Those Eskimos who supply stores need to be hunters or fishers. Most others don't. They do other kinds of work. Some run small stores. Some are guides for arctic travelers. Others have different jobs. But most Eskimo men still hunt and fish for sport. Seal and caribou are hunted most often.

Are there schools for Eskimo children?

Yes, but only in large villages. Children who live in small villages must leave their families to get an education. When they are ready to start first grade, they move to a village that has a school. Children from a few villages live together in a large building. Usually there are fewer than 30 children. At the end of the school year, they go home.

What games do Eskimos play?

Eskimos spend much of their playtime indoors, where they can keep warm. Children spend hours playing cat's cradle. Both adults and children play dominoes and a few kinds of card games. They also enjoy a game that is something like darts. They hang caribou antlers from the ceiling. Then they try to throw sticks through manmade holes in the antlers.

But the cold weather doesn't keep Eskimos from playing outdoor games, too. Naturally, the games are played in the snow or on ice. Ice hockey is a favorite. Eskimos sometimes make the puck from a walrus tusk. Long walrus bones make good hockey sticks to hit the puck with. Eskimo children like to speed downhill on sleds. Their parents enjoy dog-sled and snowmobile racing.

How People Live in the Mountains

People of the Himalayas

What is the tallest mountain in the world?

Mount Everest. It is 5½ miles (about 9 kilometers) high! That's almost 20 times as tall as the Empire State Building in New York City.

Mount Everest is one of many high peaks in Asia's Himalaya (him-uh-LAY-uh) Mountains. In that great mountain chain there are 92 peaks more than 4 miles (about 6 kilometers) high.

In what country are the Himalayas?

The Himalayas stretch across more than one country. Within this great mountain chain are three whole countries—Nepal (nuh-PAWL), Sikkim (SICK-im), and Bhutan (boo-TAHN). The Himalayas also reach into India, Pakistan, and Tibet. The Himalayas are as long from end to end as the distance between New York City and Miami, Florida.

Although the Himalayan peoples live in different countries, they are alike in many ways. They share the same kind of mountain life.

Who lives in the Himalayas?

About 20 million people live in the Himalayas. Most of them live in small villages tucked away in narrow strips of land between high mountains. We call these places valleys.

Himalayans have dark straight hair, dark eyes, and brown skin. They are short people, but most of them are strong.

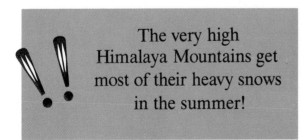

The very high Himalaya Mountains get most of their heavy snows in the summer!

Himalayan village

What are Himalayan houses like?

Most Himalayan houses are made of stone. Because glass is expensive, there are few windows. The houses stay warmer this way, too. Some houses have flat roofs. Others have roofs with a slight slant. Himalayans lay heavy stones on top of both kinds of roofs. The stones keep the roofs from blowing off in the strong mountain winds which blow all the time.

Himalayan houses are small. But they have two or three floors. The third floor is used to store food and hay. More food and wood is stored on the ground floor. In the winter it becomes a barn for animals, too. The second floor of the house has one big room. This is where the Himalayan family lives.

In cold weather the family gathers around an open fire. The fire keeps them warm and cooks their food. But the fire fills the room with smoke because Himalayan houses have no chimneys. Instead, smoke slowly escapes through the roof. No one seems to know for sure why the Himalayans have no chimneys. But we do know that they don't seem to mind the smoky air in their houses. Sometimes, though, it makes their eyes burn.

What animal is the Himalayan's best friend?

The yak is the Himalayan's best friend. It is a big animal that looks like a buffalo. Because yaks can live in rugged mountain areas, Himalayans use them for many things.

Yaks pull plows for Himalayan farmers. They can be ridden like horses, and they can carry heavy loads. Mountain women weave the yak's long hair into cloth for blankets and clothing. Yak hide, with the hair taken off, makes warm, sturdy boots.

Even the yak's horns and tail are useful. Horns are turned into musical instruments. Himalayans brush away flies with what was once a yak's tail.

The yak also supplies mountain people with meat and milk.

While looking for grass to eat, yaks have climbed close to the top of Mount Everest!

YOU BETTER SHAPE UP... YOU COULD BE REPLACED BY A YAK!

YAK! YAK! YAK!

How do Himalayans earn a living?

Some Himalayans raise sheep, goats, or yaks. A few work as guides for tourists and mountain climbers. But most are farmers. They raise cereal crops such as barley and wheat on the mountain slopes. They also grow fruits and vegetables in the valleys near their homes. Most farmers also have one or two goats, yaks, oxen, or sheep.

Yak

Couple removing dirt and husks from grain

What do Himalayan people eat?

These mountain people eat the cereal and other crops that they raise. Barley, for example, is roasted, then ground, and made into bread. Boiled or fried potatoes are a favorite food.

Yak meat is eaten fresh, or after it has been dried. Yak meat is a treat to Himalayans. They don't have it often, since they like to keep their yaks alive as long as possible. Yaks are not killed for meat until they are old. By then their meat is hard to chew. But it's a nice change from sheep and goat meat, which Himalayans eat more often.

Himalayans drink yak milk, and they make cheese and butter from it. Himalayans of all ages drink tea to which salt and yak butter have been added.

Do Himalayans have stores?

Most Himalayan villages do not have stores. The village families grow or make most of the things they need.

Once a year a Himalayan family may travel to a market town. There people from all over the mountain area gather to buy and sell. Some markets are outdoors. Others are in a building.

Family members take with them the sweaters, blankets, and other things they have made. At the market they trade for whatever they need. That might be tea, spices, or metal tools. Because they trade one thing for another, many mountain people do not use money.

Woman weaving cloth to take to the market

118

Do Himalayan children go to school?

Some do and some don't. Only large villages and towns have schools. The mountains make it impossible for children to travel back and forth from one village to another every day. Children from small villages must leave home for a while to go to school. But not very many do. So a lot of children never learn to read and write. Instead they learn to plant crops, weave, cook, and do other practical things. Children from large towns learn reading, writing, and arithmetic, and some go on to college in other countries.

Himalayan school children

Travelers walking through the snow

How do Himalayan people travel from place to place?

They usually walk. They walk even when they are going to a place many miles away. Building a road across a high mountain is very hard. So few roads have been built in the Himalayas.

Mountain travelers walk along steep, rocky trails. They cross rivers on rickety bridges. Sometimes travelers have to go through a narrow pass, or opening, between mountain peaks. They can do this only when the snow is not very deep.

When they travel, mountain people carry whatever they need for the trip. If they have many bundles, they load them on yaks or other animals.

What do Himalayan people do if they get sick?

Many Himalayans believe that illness is caused by evil spirits. When these Himalayans are ill, they call in a shaman. This shaman is much like the shaman of the Amazon rain forest. Both try to cure sickness by dealing with spirits as well as natural medicine.

Himalayans believe that a shaman can ask good spirits to drive out evil spirits. Then the sick person should get well. But sometimes he doesn't. Then the Himalayans say the evil spirits were stronger than the good spirits.

Many Himalayans who live in small isolated villages never visit a modern doctor. As a result, some of them die of diseases a doctor could cure.

Shaman dancing

120

Is there really an "Abominable Snowman"?

Nobody knows for sure. There have been many reports of a shaggy creature who lives in the Himalayas. The creature is reported to be half human and half ape. Some people say it has a high-pitched scream and a bad smell. Its feet are supposed to point backward. The Himalayans' name for the Abominable Snowman is yeti (YET-ee).

The mysterious yeti is said to roam the Himalayas at night. A few people claim to have seen a yeti. But they cannot prove that they did see one. Others claim that they have seen yeti tracks in the snow. But we can't be sure that a yeti made the tracks.

Maybe one day mountain climbers will capture a yeti. Or perhaps they will be able to take a picture of one. Then we will know for sure if the yeti really exists.

 Instead of celebrating their real birthdays, all people in the country of Bhutan become a year older on New Year's Day!

How People Live in the Desert

People of the Sahara

What is a desert?

A desert is an area of very dry land. Rain almost never falls there. Only a few plants can grow in a desert, and animals have a hard time finding water to drink.

Most deserts are hot and sandy. But others are rocky and cold.

There are deserts in many parts of the world.

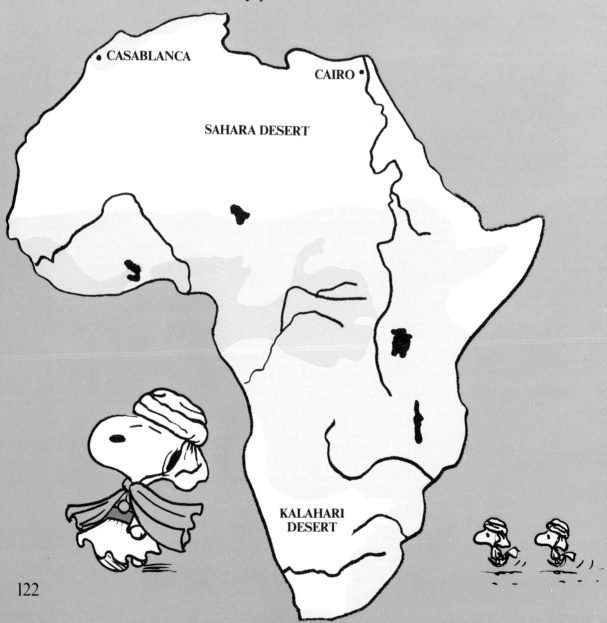

CASABLANCA

CAIRO

SAHARA DESERT

KALAHARI DESERT

What is the world's biggest desert?

The Sahara (suh-HARE-uh) Desert in Northern Africa. It is about the same size as the United States.

Sahara means both "desert" and "wilderness" in Arabic—the language of some of the Saharan people. A wilderness is a place that people have not yet changed and used. The modern Sahara Desert has some towns, highways, factories, mines, and oil fields. But most of it is still a wilderness. So living there is very hard.

Some parts of the Sahara are sandy. Other parts are rocky. But all parts of it are hot and sunny during the day and cool at night.

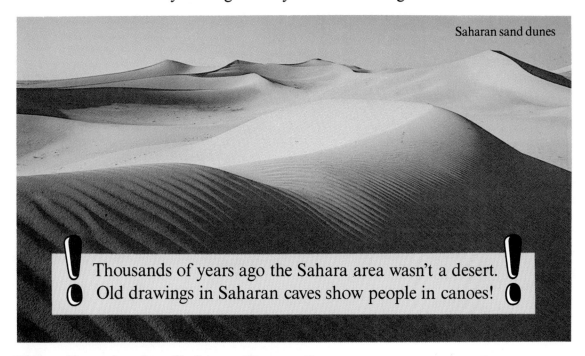

Saharan sand dunes

! Thousands of years ago the Sahara area wasn't a desert.
! Old drawings in Saharan caves show people in canoes!

Who lives in the Sahara Desert?

There are three tribes of people that live in the Sahara. The Moors live in the west. The Tuareg (TWAH-reg) live in the central part. The Tebu (TEH-boo) live in the east.

Each tribe speaks a different language and has its own customs. But because they all live in the desert, their way of life is much the same.

How do desert people get water?

From an oasis (oh-AY-sis). Even a desert has underground water in some places. These places are called oases. At oases the water may rise to the surface and form a spring or water hole. If it doesn't, people can dig a well to reach the water. In the Sahara Desert there are 90 big oases.

Before desert people leave an oasis, they fill goatskin bags with water. Some also fill round rubber tubes found inside old car and truck tires. In this way they have water while they travel.

How do desert people get food?

Some people live at an oasis and grow crops for food there. They use ditches or pipes to run water from a well or spring to the crops. This system is called irrigation (ir-uh-GAY-shun).

Other desert people travel from one spot in the desert to another. They raise herds of animals for meat and clothing. They buy fruits and vegetables at a market whenever they pass through a town. These people are called nomads.

124

Why do nomads travel from one spot to another?

Most nomads keep traveling to find food and water for their herds of camels, sheep, or goats.

Animals quickly eat the few plants that grow in a desert pasture. Then the nomads have to find a new pasture—sometimes miles and miles away. To reach it they have to travel for at least two days. Sometimes they must travel for two weeks! When they get to a new pasture, they unpack and set up a camp. But soon they will move on again.

Nomads on their way to a new camp

How do nomads carry all their supplies?

On the backs of their camels. Camels are great helpers to desert nomads. Camels' soft, wide feet don't sink deeply into sand. So they can walk easily in the desert. Camels can carry heavy loads. They can also go without drinking water for a long time. Seven to ten days is about their limit when traveling across the desert. And when there is little food, camels can live on the fat that is stored in their humps.

Because camels are good at carrying supplies, some desert people use them to make a living. The camels carry supplies across the desert to be sold. People who sell things are called merchants. Desert merchants often travel together in groups called caravans (CARE-uh-vanz). A caravan of merchants can protect its members against robbers better than a few people traveling alone can.

In the winter, a camel that does not work or travel can go without water for as long as two months!

How else do camels help desert people?

Camels not only CARRY supplies—they ARE supplies themselves! Nomads drink camel's milk and eat camel meat. From camel skins, nomads make leather for tents. From camel's hair they make wool clothes.

Camels also carry people on their backs. When desert travelers are tired, they can saddle up a camel like a horse. Then they can ride across the dessert.

Camel loaded with supplies

Do nomads take their houses with them when they move?

Yes! Most nomads live in tents made of camel skins. The tents are held up with poles. Some nomads make their own poles from trees found at oases. Other nomads buy theirs from passing caravans. At moving time, they fold up their tents. They can then easily load the tents onto camels.

The objects in nomad houses get packed up, too. Nomads don't use the same kind of furniture as we do. Chairs, tables, and beds are heavy and bulky. A camel couldn't carry them around the desert easily. Instead, nomads use mats that they weave from palm branches. Nomads sit on mats, sleep on mats, and use mats as tables.

Nomad family sitting on mats in front of their tent

 From years of walking through sand, the soles of nomads' feet become tough. Some can put their feet in a low fire and not feel it!

Do nomads take baths while traveling across the desert?

No! Traveling nomads must use all the water they have for drinking and cooking. They have to wait until they settle at another oasis before they can take a bath. This can sometimes be as long as two weeks.

Desert market

Are there towns in the Sahara?

Yes, but most of them are small. And all are near water.

In a desert town, people live in houses made from mud bricks dried in the sun. At the center of the town is usually an outdoor market. There the people buy food and supplies. Some larger desert towns also have stores, restaurants, and hotels.

Nomads sometimes travel to a desert town to visit the market. There they often sell or trade some of their animals. Sometimes they spend time with friends who live in the town.

Do nomads go to school?

Some do. Many of the governments of Saharan countries send teachers to nomad camps. So people learn to read and write.

128

Boy learning to read

What kind of food is served at a desert meal?

When desert families have guests, they often serve sheep or lamb that has been roasted over an open fire. On ordinary days, desert cooks boil the meat of a sheep, a lamb, or a chicken. Chickpeas and cut-up vegetables such as carrots, onions, and beans go into the same pot. Cooks also add pepper and other spices. A desert family eats a cereal called couscous (KOOS-koos), too. It is usually served in a large bowl with the meat and vegetables.

Family eating millet

Camel cheese and camel butter are also popular foods. Camel cheese is made from camel's milk. But camel butter isn't. Camel butter is the fat from the camel's hump. People smear it on certain foods. Or else they dip their fingers in it and eat it plain.

Desert people like to drink sweet tea with their meals. But sometimes they drink goat's milk or camel's milk.

A pile of sand formed by the wind is called a sand dune. There is one in the Sahara Desert that is taller than the highest building in New York City!

Is all of the Sahara covered with sand?

No. Most of the Sahara Desert does NOT have sand on it! In some areas tiny pebbles called gravel cover the ground. In other places there is only bare rock. The middle of the big desert has the most sand.

Is there anything under the sand and rock of the Sahara?

Yes. Oil! Oil companies have found large amounts of valuable oil under the sand and rock of Algeria (al-JEER-ee-uh) and Libya (LIB-ee-uh). Algeria and Libya are two countries in the northern part of the Sahara Desert.

Oil companies have started bringing up the oil from under the desert. Pipe lines carry the oil from the desert to African cities on the Mediterranean (med-ih-tuh-RAY-nee-un) Sea. This sea is just north of Africa.

From the cities the oil is loaded into big ships called tankers. It is then shipped to places all over the world. Some of it comes to the United States.

Has oil changed life in the Sahara Desert?

Yes. Many Libyans and Algerians have stopped living as nomads. They now work in the oil fields. Instead of moving from place to place, they live in new towns near their jobs.

Because of the oil business, roads have been built across the desert. Trucks carry some of the loads that camels once carried.

But in the rest of the Sahara Desert, life goes on as it has for many hundreds of years.

130

How People Live in the Lowlands
The Rice Farmers of Asia

MILK MUST BE THE MOST COMMON FOOD IN THE WORLD.

NO, I THINK IT'S RICE.

OF COURSE, GIVEN A PREFERENCE, ONE WOULD MAKE IT JELLY DOUGHNUTS, EVERY TIME.

Which is the most commonly eaten food in the world?

Charlie Brown is right. More people eat rice than any other food. It is the main food of about half the world's people.

In Asia, rice is one food that almost everybody eats. Asians depend on rice for starches that give their bodies energy.

131

Where does rice grow?

Rice grows in warm, wet places, including the southern part of the United States. Usually land good for growing rice is low. More rice is grown in Asia than anywhere else. China, India, Indonesia (in-duh-NEE-zhuh), Bangladesh (BANG-luh-desh), Japan, and Thailand (TIE-land) are the six Asian countries that grow the most rice.

Do many people live in the six main rice-growing countries of Asia?

Yes. Nearly two billion people live there. This is slightly less than half the people in the whole world! And the number of people in these countries is growing very fast. In some areas there, people are already terribly crowded together.

How can people find enough land to farm in such crowded places?

Most of Asia's rice growers farm small pieces of land. The land on which rice grows is called a paddy. Some paddies are no bigger than a football field.

But there are many of these small paddies. Together they produce a lot of rice. The six main rice-growing countries produce about 260 million tons (236 million metric tons) of rice a year.

! Paddy means "rice field." So when you say "rice paddy" you are saying "rice-rice field."

HOW WOULD IT SOUND IF I CHANGED MY NAME TO PATTY RICEFIELD OR RICE PATTYFIELD OR RICE RICEFIELD OR...

GOOD GRIEF!

What animal helps Asians grow rice?

The water buffalo. It is a large, strong animal with big horns. In spite of its size, the water buffalo is a gentle animal. A child can safely lead one as it works.

When a rice farmer plows his paddy, a water buffalo usually pulls the plow. The plow makes ditches in the earth. Then rice seeds are planted in them. From the seeds, stalks grow a few feet high. On the stalks grow the grains which people eat. When the grains are ripe, the stalks are cut down. They are put on a cart that is pulled by a water buffalo. The stalks are then spread on the ground. The water buffalo walks over them. This forces the grains from the stalks.

Water buffalo pulling plow in Indonesia

133

Do rice farmers use any farm machines?

Most paddies are too small for the rice farmer to use farm machines. Instead, the work is done by hand. All the family members help to plant the rice and pull weeds from the paddy. When the rice is ripe, they cut it with sharp knives.

A few rice farmers have begun to use tractors to pull their plows. Because the paddies are so small, a few families share one tractor. But even these families do most of their work with their hands.

Flooded rice fields in the Philippines

Rice is grown in flooded fields. This means that the rice farm family often works in ankle-deep water!

How do rice farmers flood their fields?

Water to flood rice fields usually comes from rivers. Man-made waterways called canals carry the water to narrow ditches. The ditches carry the water to the paddies. Farmers build gates of wood or mud to stop the flow when enough water is in the paddy. Dikes hold the water in. Dikes are low walls made from the soil of the paddy. Most rice-growing areas have a lot of rain during the growing season. This makes it easier to keep the paddies flooded. But from time to time, the farmer has to add more water anyway.

134

Farmers cleaning rice grains

 Some Indonesian people believe that rats and mice brought rice to their land. So they let these animals eat as much rice from the fields as they like!

HEY, STUPID CAT, HOW DOES THAT GRAB YOU?

What kind of houses do Asian rice farmers build?

Many build houses high up on stilts. This keeps them from being flooded during heavy rains. The stilts and the walls of the houses are made of wood or bamboo. The roofs are made of straw or strips of metal.

Most houses are small. Sometimes they have only one room. But almost every house has a porch.

The houses have windows—but no glass or screens. The rice farmers are poor and cannot afford them. So insects fly right inside the houses. And there are many flies, mosquitoes, and other insects in the rice-growing countries. During bad weather the people cover their windows with wooden shutters.

Where do rice farmers build their houses?

Rice farmers build their houses in villages. They do not live right next to their fields as American farmers do. Each morning the rice farmers walk from the village to their paddies. At the end of the day they walk home again.

In some rice-growing areas there are few roads. Rivers and canals go to more places than roads do. Many rice farmers live in villages close to a river or canal. These people usually travel in a rowboat.

135

Rice farmers who live near a canal use its waters for bathing, cooking, brushing their teeth, and washing their clothes!

Philippine school children working in field next to their school

Are there schools for rice farmers' children?

Japanese teacher helping child with his writing

Only in some places. In China and Japan there are schools for the children of ALL rice-farming families. But in the other leading rice-growing countries, only the largest villages have schools. In some places teachers or older students visit middle-sized villages for a few months at a time. They teach children to read, write, and do arithmetic. But many children who grow up in small, poor villages never learn to read and write.

Where do rice farmers go shopping?

In the nearest town. Few small villages have stores of their own.

For some rice-growing families, going shopping means taking a boat ride on a river or a canal. For other families it means walking a few miles. In some places they can ride at least part of the way in a small bus.

Families often take along something to sell at the town market.

Shoppers in Thailand traveling by boat to stores that line the canals

What do rice farmers eat?

It should be no surprise that their main food is rice. Asian rice farmers boil most of the rice that they eat. But they also eat it steamed or fried. Sometimes they cover the rice with a sauce made from boiled fish.

Some rice-growing families also raise and eat sweet potatoes, yams, beans, peas, or other vegetables. They might have a few fruit trees, some chickens, and a pig. Now and then they go fishing, or they buy a fish. But the poorest rice farmers have little to eat besides rice.

Market in Indonesia

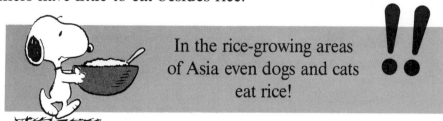

In the rice-growing areas of Asia even dogs and cats eat rice!

How healthy is rice?

Rice is full of B vitamins and iron. For a very long time, people in the United States used to throw out the healthiest part of the rice—the bran. The part they ate had none of the vitamins or iron in it.

What we call rice is only part of the rice plant—the grains. Around each rice grain grow a few thin brown coatings called bran. Rice bran is much like the bran used to make bran cereals. But cereal bran comes from wheat—not rice. Around the bran coatings is another coating called the hull. Before people eat rice, they usually take off the bran and the hull. Today, most rice is soaked in hot water before the coatings are taken off. This transfers the vitamins and iron into the white part of the rice grain.

New rice

Ripe rice

Rice grains

Do rice farmers' villages have doctors?

Most villages do not have doctors. A family of rice farmers may live their whole lives without ever visiting a doctor. But some are visited by a shaman.

Many of Asia's rice farmers believe that they are surrounded by spirits. They think that spirits live in every field and every house. To these rice farmers, illness means that the spirits are angry. When they are sick, they do what the Himalayans and Brazilian Indians do. They call in a shaman. He tells them how to make the spirits happy again.

138

How People Live in the City

What is a city?

A city is a town that has grown very big. Many people live and work there. People usually move to a city from farms and small villages or towns. Some come there to find better or more interesting work. Others come to find more interesting people. Cities often attract people from many different places in the world.

139

Which cities have the most people?

New York City, in the United States, Tokyo (TOE-kee-oh), in Japan, Mexico City, in Mexico, and Shanghai (SHANG-hi), in the People's Republic of China, have the most people. Which of these has the most is hard to say. The numbers keep changing. But more than seven million people live in each of these cities.

Why are many big cities near water?

Long ago there were no cars, trains, or airplanes. There were just a few rough roads for horses and carriages. So the easiest way to travel long distances was by ship.

Cities grew up near oceans and rivers. Travelers got on or off ships there. People could find jobs there. Traders moved there to buy and sell things that ships carried. Some workers moved to cities to make things that were sent away on ships. Others found jobs in hotels, banks, and stores. As a result, the cities grew larger and larger.

Of the world's four largest cities, only Mexico City is not on a river or ocean.

Mexico City

Tokyo

New York City skyline

Why do some cities have subways?

To help people get around the city. Subways carry many people at once. If all these people were driving cars through the city streets, traffic would be jammed up all the time. There would be even fewer parking spaces than there are now.

Subways are electric railways that run through tunnels under some cities. They carry people quickly from one part of the city to another. They are fast because there is no other traffic under the streets. Some subway trains stop every few blocks. So people don't have far to walk when they get off the train. Usually an elevator, a stairway, or a moving stairway called an escalator (ES-kuh-lay-tur) leads from the station to the street.

Sixty-seven of the world's cities have subways. Of these, New York City's subway has the most riders—in some years as many as two billion!

The world's largest apartment building is in London, England. It has apartments for 1,220 families!

BLIMEY!

What kinds of houses are there in a city?

Many city people live in either apartment houses or row houses.

Apartment houses are buildings that have been divided into groups of rooms called apartments. Each apartment is a home for one person or a family. Some apartment buildings are very large. Hundreds of people live in them.

A row house is one in a row of small houses. Usually just one family lives in each house. All the houses are joined together, and they all look alike. The row of houses may be as long as a city block.

Cities have apartment houses and row houses to save space. Cities have a lot of people, but they usually have little land. Everything must be crowded together. Apartment houses take up air space instead of using up more ground space. Row houses use more land than apartment houses. But they use less land than separate one-family houses.

In every city there are at least a few separate houses for one family. These houses usually cost a lot of money.

World Trade Center towers

Which city has the most tall buildings?

New York. There's no way to tell how many tall buildings there are. The number keeps growing all the time.

The Empire State Building was the tallest in New York until the World Trade Center was built. The Trade Center is 1,350 feet (404 meters) high.

How can a city sink?

When water is pumped out from under a city, the city slowly sinks.

The soil under Mexico city has a lot of water in it. The city gets some of its drinking water by pumping it out of the soil. As the water level in the soil gets lower, the soil gets lower too. And so do the streets and buildings on top of the soil.

Parts of Tokyo are also sinking. The sinking areas were once all water. The water was filled in with land to make more room for people to live. Water for factories to use is pumped out from under this man-made land. So the land sinks. These areas are so low that they get flooded whenever there are heavy rains.

> Since 1900, parts of Mexico City have sunk as much as 25 feet (more than 7 meters)!

Which is the oldest city in the world?

Probably Jericho (JER-uh-koe). It is in Jordan near Israel. Groups of people were living there about 7,000 or 8,000 years ago!

If you have heard Bible stories, you probably know something about Jericho. The story is that Joshua and his men surrounded the city. They blew trumpets and yelled until the walls around Jericho tumbled down.

By digging under the earth, scientists have found ruins of Jericho as it was a long time ago.

143

Did all large cities grow from small towns?

Most of them did. But some cities were planned and built as cities. These places were never small towns. They started out big. Factories, stores, apartment buildings, and offices were built as part of the plan.

Planned cities are the easiest to get around in. Streets are laid out neatly. Buildings and stores aren't jumbled together the way they are in many cities that grew without any plan. Planned cities are called new towns. Columbia, Maryland, and Reston, Virginia, are two new towns.

Another example of a planned city is Brasília (brah-SEEL-yuh), in Brazil. It was built to be that country's capital.

Brasília was designed in the shape of a large cross. You can see the cross when you look down at Brasília from an airplane. All around the city are green fields. Wide roads that lead to the city have been built through the fields.

SOMEDAY, I'LL LOOK IN CITIES AROUND THE WORLD FOR HAPPINESS, BUT I'LL PROBABLY NEVER FIND IT...

THEN, AFTER I'VE LOOKED IN EVERY CITY, I'LL RETURN HOME.

AND WHEN YOU RETURN HOME, YOU'LL FIND THE VERY HAPPINESS THAT WAS THERE ALL ALONG! IS THAT WHAT YOU'RE TRYING TO SAY?

NO, MAYBE I'LL FIND THAT STUPID LITTLE PINK BRACELET I LOST YESTERDAY!

 !! Brasília has the world's widest street. It is wider than two and a half football fields placed end to end! **!!**

O.K. I'LL GO TO PARIS WITH YOU, BUT I'VE GOT TO GET HOME IN TIME FOR DINNER

Which is the best city in the world?

There are so many wonderful cities in the world that no one can truly say which is the best.

Index